CROSS-COUNTRY RIDING

CROSS-COUNTRY RIDING

Preparation and training for both horse and rider

Sarah Cotton

B.T. Batsford Ltd · London

First published 1994

Typeset by Servis Filmsetting Ltd, Manchester
and printed in Great Britain by
Butler and Tanner, Frome, Somerset

Published by
B.T. Batsford Ltd
4 Fitzhardinge Street
London W1H 0AH

A CIP catalogue record for this book is available
from the British Library

ISBN 0 7134 7120 4

CONTENTS

ACKNOWLEDGEMENTS

I would like to thank Josh Bates for his wonderfully placid temperament, and for putting up with me during the frustrating times caused by the writing of this book – I am sorry I have been so anti-social.

Thanks to Sue Sale for painstakingly typing the first manuscript; Clifford and Ann Leftly for their help with the typing and the word processor; Jonathen Benson for all his help with the computer; H.N.D. Horse Studies students from Writtle College for all their help with the typing; Louise Davies and Chris Caden Parker for printing the manuscript; Lea Marshall and Lisa Price for drawing some of the references for illustrations; Rosalind Cecil for her enthusiasm and for finding eleven hours' work that I had 'lost' in the word processor; Jane and Jeremy Houghton-Brown and Jo and George Hodges for all their help and support over the last seven years; Sarah Pilliner for all her unselfish help, support and work during the sorting of the original manuscript, and her husband, Simon Hamlyn, for providing us with good food and drink at the end of each day's work; Sam Wycherley, Sarah Pilliner, Norman, Morag and her daughter Megan for being such good models; Joanna Prestwich for taking the photographs; and Somerford Park Farm for letting us use the cross-country fences.

My thanks also go to my parents for buying me my first pony and for their enthusiastic support over the last twenty-five years, and most thanks are due to Mrs Moo (Morag) for being such a wonderful horse and for providing the Cotton family with so many unforgettable times. Without her, I would not have learned as much as I have done, so really it is her fault that I have written this book!

All technical line illustrations are by Carole Vincer, and the decorative line illustrations are by Gabrielle Ceriden Morse.

All photographs are by Joanna Prestwich, except the jacket photograph and 57 on page 158, which are by Kit Houghton.

INTRODUCTION

The last thirty years have seen a great rise in the popularity of the competition horse, with equestrian sports ranging from polo to dressage, and show jumping to endurance riding. One of the greatest growth areas is in all forms of cross-country riding.

Whether it is in eventing, hunter trials, team chasing or part of a horse trial, cross-country riding is exhilarating, and demands bravery in both horse and rider. It has been argued that the potential risks involved in galloping over solid fences allow horse and rider to develop a unique rapport based on mutual trust and empathy. There is certainly nothing to beat the euphoric feeling of having successfully negotiated an imposing series of fences knowing that your horse has tried his utmost, particularly when you were filled with nervous anticipation beforehand.

In the past, the British relied upon young people learning to ride across country in the hunting field, and this is an excellent place to learn, particularly when backed up with Pony Club tuition. Now there is a new generation of rider: people may learn to ride later in life, or live in a town with no access to riding areas other than arenas or schools, while the weekend rider may not have the desire, or indeed the finances, to go foxhunting.

To be successful across country, these riders need to learn the techniques of jumping at speed over fixed obstacles, in just the same way that a discipline such as dressage must be learned – it is rarely something that simply comes naturally.

This book aims to teach you how to be a successful competitor, starting with the very basics of training your horse on the flat and over fences before cross-country courses are even attempted. It is vital to start off slowly and proceed in a logical fashion, so that confidence and technique grow side by side. All forms of riding demand firm foundations on which to work, and the margin for error caused by loss of balance or an incorrect approach is very small when riding across country.

There is advice on cross-country schooling for inexperienced horses, and detailed descriptions of the types of fences that will be encountered on cross-country courses are accompanied by series of photographs showing the right way and wrong way to approach and jump fences, so that you can learn by other people's mistakes. There is a stage-by-stage guide to walking the

The young horse jumping off a bank. He has lengthened his head and neck considerably and has jumped out a long way, a little too freely. The rider's position is good, although the lower legs could be a little further forward

course, whether it is at a hunter trials, or a one- or three-day event, and advice on how to ride the course and the relationship you should have with your horse.

I hope that the logical and practical approach used throughout the book will allow both experienced riders and those new to the sport, along with their horses, to enjoy riding safely and successfully across country for many years to come.

Part 1
TRAINING THE HORSE AND RIDER

1
TRAINING ON THE FLAT

The cross-country horse benefits greatly from correct training on the flat, as it will help him to carry himself and you with the maximum of ease and the minimum of effort. As he is required to gallop over all types of terrain in different conditions, and to jump fences as well, he will not last long if these tasks are stressful and signs of wear and tear become noticeable (1).

The horse's conformation means that he carries two-thirds of his weight on the forehand. This is ideal for horses living in the wild, as they can balance themselves while performing all their tasks, but problems arise when a rider's weight is added. The horse is still expected to remain in balance, while galloping up and down hills and jumping fences as well. For him to achieve this with a rider, he has to learn to re-distribute his weight and adapt his posture so that he remains in balance at all times, while the body structures have to develop so that they can support the re-distributed weight. This development and re-balancing allows the horse to become an equine athlete.

The balanced horse will cover the ground and jump using his energy economically. His action should show good co-ordination and be free from stiffness or discomfort, and the impression should be of light and balanced movement. You can then communicate more effectively with the horse in terms of direction, pace, tempo, balance and rhythm and, being the one who has walked the course, can present the horse at each fence with all the ingredients necessary for a safe and confident jump. The correctly trained and developed horse will suffer less of the wear and tear associated with cross-country riding, which will prolong and enhance his competitive career.

The young horse

In the initial stages of training, the young horse should be taught to carry himself and you at the basic paces on good, even ground. He should accept the bit with a relaxed jaw and a quiet mouth, and have a good, rounded outline (fig.1). You should be able to ride the horse through simple turns and changes of direction, keeping his forward movement channelled between your legs and hands. At first, the

1 (Right) Good training on the flat teaches the cross-country horse to carry himself and, later, to negotiate fences with the minimum of effort, reducing the chances of injury and stress. This young horse has jumped out a long way from the bank and may land heavily, which could cause jarring. With experience, he will learn to judge fences more economically and not to over-jump in this way

Fig. 1 Establishing a good outline. The horse becomes more engaged as the development increases. The hindlegs step under the body to create impulsion, the head and neck carriage is more condensed and the forehand becomes lighter

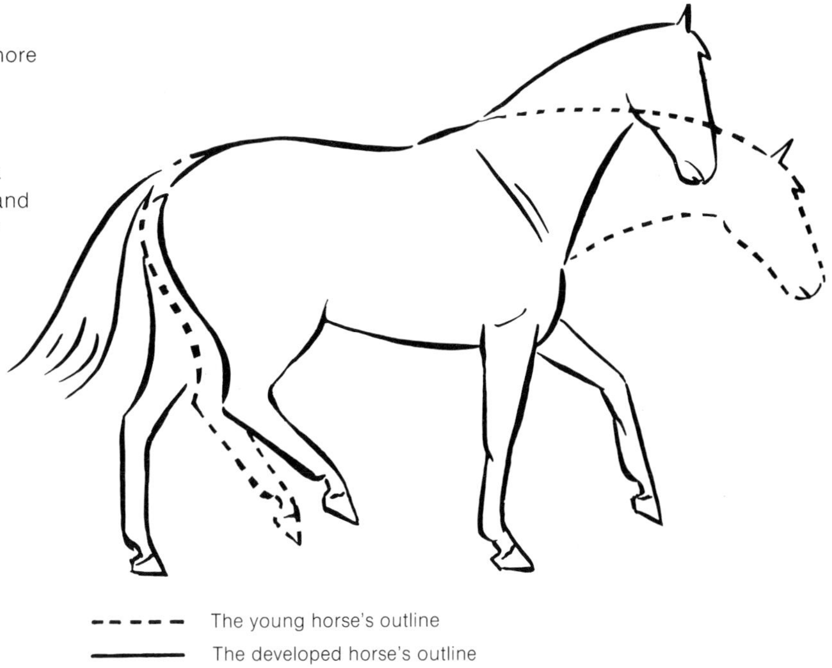

- - - - - The young horse's outline
————— The developed horse's outline

impulsion must be equal to the horse's stage of development as, if too much impulsion is introduced before the horse has learned to carry himself and your weight, it will lead to tension and resentment. In practical terms, this means that the horse will have to lean on the rein as a means of support, as he will not have learned how to control the impulsion with his hindquarters.

Transitions

Transitions are a very useful way of helping the horse to re-balance himself in order to cope with your weight and the movements he is being taught. Initially, he will use his forelegs to propel himself forward through the paces, and for the downward transitions the majority of his weight will be on the forehand. As the horse finds it difficult to adjust his balance in the early stages, he will often try to lean on the rein as a means of support. This is by far the easiest solution to his problem, but using his forehand to control himself will increase the wear and tear on his forelegs and feet, and may lead to problems at a later stage.

Transitions in walk and trot

As an exercise, start by establishing a well-balanced trot: the horse should show a fairly regular gait, have a consistent outline and hold the bit in his mouth without leaning on your hands. He must show a uniform amount of bend through his body from the poll to the tail, and the imprints of the hind feet should be in the same line as the imprints of the front feet. Rising trot is easier for the horse initially, as he does not have to cope with your weight constantly on his back.

You can then start to ask the horse to think about making a transition to walk.

By slowing down the rising, keeping your shoulders up and keeping the horse relaxed and quiet on the end of the rein, it is possible to make the downward transition. If you remain in rising trot, it helps the horse to stay soft in the back, and therefore avoids the temptation of him leaning against the rein to support himself. Keeping your lower legs in contact with the horse's sides teaches him to slow his hindlegs down first, controlling the transition so that the forehand can stay light and relaxed and the horse can remain in balance.

For the upward transition from walk to trot, keep the horse soft, relaxed and on the end of the rein without his head and neck becoming short and hollow. Use your legs and seat to encourage him to activate his hindquarters and create impulsion. Try not to let the horse pull you forward out of position so that he can just shuffle into trot with his forelegs. Always maintain your position, which will help the horse to keep his outline, and then ask him to go into trot by using your legs in a series of nudges. If the trot becomes too fast, the horse will lose his balance and will shorten and hollow his outline to try to counteract the problem. If this happens, slow him down by sitting up and keeping your shoulders back, and then very gently use a series of half-halts which will act as a restriction to the forward movement. Do not use a rigid hand contact, as this will encourage the horse to set his jaw against you, but give and take with the rein, using an almost invisible aid. The aim is to slow down the speed of the rhythm (the tempo), not to break it.

At first the horse will find it difficult to keep the outline during these transitions, but if he is given time to adjust his balance so that he can perform them, he will soon learn to stay soft in the hand with a long, slightly elevated and rounded neck and a supple body. A good neck position helps the balance. If the horse puts his head down, he will fall on to his forehand and will expect you to hold him up, whereas, if his neck is raised, more weight can be transferred over his hindquarters. In addition, the neck must always be slightly rounded from the withers to the poll, not flat and hollow, or the back will hollow, preventing the hindlegs from stepping under the body **(fig. 2)**.

Always make these transitions on a curve until the horse becomes well-balanced, as straight lines require dexterity. Imagine the small child learning to ride his bicycle: it takes him some time to master cycling in a straight line, yet a continual curve is always easier to manage. A horse is the same, so do not expect him to achieve perfection immediately, and allow him time to find his balance. It is also vital that the horse does not become confused, so you must apply clear aids and know that the horse understands what you want him to do. It is better to progress a little at a time, as the horse, like a young child, does not have a very long concentration span. As you teach him new exercises, it will therefore take

some time before he can perform them with ease. The ultimate goal is to be able to perform the transitions in quick succession, anywhere in the school: on or off the track, on a straight line or on a curve.

Transitions in trot and canter

It takes time for a horse to master cantering on a given leg. Start by working in trot on a large circle. Check that the trot is going forward in balance, and open the inside rein to encourage the horse to keep coming round on the line of the circle. Apply the leg aids for canter, and then encourage the horse to make the transition. If this does not happen immediately, maintain the bend, stay on the circle and, with a little help from a more persistent leg aid and the use of the voice, the horse will soon learn to go forward to canter.

At this stage, either sit very lightly with the weight in the lower legs, or keep your weight out of the saddle. Do not lean forward, as this will put more weight on the forehand and the horse will just go faster in trot, and will not actually canter, especially if you waver off the line of the

Fig. 2 An incorrect outline. The horse has a high head and neck carriage, a hollow back and trailing hocks, causing a lack of impulsion

circle. Canter for short periods initially, and remember the young child on his bicycle wobbling instead of achieving straight lines. If you experience difficulties with the transition to canter, introduce a pole or small log. Trot to the pole, and pick up canter as you reach it.

To canter like this on a given leg, introduce the exercise on the circle so that the continual turning encourages the horse to pick up the correct lead, but use a circle of no less than 20 metres (66 ft) in diameter or the horse will not be able to keep his balance. This exercise can also be used while lungeing the horse, and, if the voice command 'canter' is learned, it can be useful when the horse is being taught to canter when ridden.

For a downward transition from canter to trot, bring the horse on to the large circle. Having checked the acceptance of the bit, the outline, the bend and the softness, think of slowing the tempo (the speed of the rhythm). This can be done by 'thinking slower' with your mind, sitting up with your upper body and keeping your shoulders up and back. Keep the contact with your lower legs to encourage the horse to keep cantering, even with a slower tempo. Check that he remains soft at the poll and relaxed and soft in the mouth, and let him come back to trot in his own time. Using your voice will also help.

If the horse tries to trot by leaning on the rein, sit up and maintain the pressure with your legs to encourage him to slow the speed by slowing down the hindlegs. If you have lost the softness, feel the bit in the horse's mouth by squeezing your fingers so that he relaxes his jaw again. If he insists on lowering his neck so that the weight is transferred over his forehand, use a neck strap and hold on to this to assist with the downward transitions. A slow, balanced canter will produce a slow, balanced trot, so always prepare the canter as much as possible before making the downward transition. If the horse continually rushes off once you are in trot, make a transition to walk as soon as possible, then go forward to trot and canter, then back to trot and walk again. If you execute a number of these transitions in quick succession, the horse will realize that there is no point in rushing off in trot if there is a transition to walk coming shortly.

The goal is to be able to execute these transitions at any place and at any time. Teach your horse how to execute these transitions on the circle, and, when you think they are good, see if you can move on to performing them anywhere and at any time – providing of course that you have prepared the horse correctly beforehand. At this stage, work for approximately ten minutes at a time and then rest by walking on a long rein.

POINTS TO REMEMBER

- Be generous with your praise and always be patient, as it will take time for you both to achieve perfection.
- It is better to work mainly in rising trot, especially during the working-in period, to encourage the horse to be soft and to swing through his back, but alternating the trot between rising and sitting will teach the horse to accept your weight.
- Be aware of when the horse is unsure of your commands, or is just being idle.
- Be specific and clear with your aids, and always give yourself plenty of time to prepare the horse for the next movement.
- A fresh, tired, tense or anxious horse cannot learn correctly.
- From time to time, it is helpful to have an experienced person on the ground whose advice you respect.

Working within each pace

The next stage in transition work is to do some exercises to improve the quality of the paces and the suppleness and straightness. The horse must be taught to move away from the leg, as a means of keeping him straight and stopping him from falling in or out. When performed on the circle, this also helps the horse to achieve a greater degree of balance. When moving the horse away from the inside leg (leg-yielding) on the circle, he must step under his body to a greater extent with the inside hindleg to achieve greater engagement and submission.

The horse should show a small amount of inside bend which should remain consistent throughout the exercise, and he should not rush away from the leg when asked to move out on to a larger circle. If this happens, use a series of half-halts to explain to the horse that he is supposed to move forward and sideways, and not just forward in a faster tempo. Ensure that the inside bend of the head and neck does not increase, as the horse will then become crooked with too much weight on the outside shoulder. Even though the horse is learning to move sideways away from the leg, he should remain on the line of the circle with the hindquarters following the same track as the forehand (fig. 3).

To return to a smaller circle, move the horse away from the outside leg and spiral back down to a smaller circle. The horse should bend in the direction in which he is travelling: on the left rein he should show a little left bend, and on the right rein a little right bend, from the poll to the tail. He should remain soft and relaxed in his mouth and body, and the tempo and balance should not alter.

Start by teaching this exercise in walk, and establish a 10 metre (33 ft) circle before asking the horse to move away from your inside leg. Finish the exercise by spiralling back on to the ten-metre circle. When executing this movement in trot, a 12 metre (39 ft) circle is an ideal size from which to work. In order to execute this movement in canter, it must first be possible to ride a 15 metre (49 ft) circle without loss of rhythm or balance.

Leg-yielding can also be performed on the straight line by riding straight down the three-quarter line and leg-yielding back to the track. The horse must remain parallel to the track, and must not rush back to it by stepping over too quickly or by leading with his quarters or shoulders. The tempo must remain constant, as any quickening of the rhythm can result in the horse falling on to his forehand, which makes the exercise invalid. For this exercise to be useful when performed from canter, it must be possible to ride the horse down the three-quarter line without loss of rhythm or balance before the leg-yielding is even attempted.

For a horse to be successful across country, he must be capable of condensing or extending his outline and stride when the terrain or the nature of the fence demands it. A useful exercise is to lengthen and shorten the stride within the pace. This will help the horse to carry more weight over his hindquarters, and he will start to bend his stifle, hock and fetlock joints to a greater degree. The forehand will become lighter and you will find the horse more obedient and submissive.

Start by establishing a good working trot, with the horse moving freely forward with a supple outline, and going forward from the leg into the hand. Think of slowing the trot, as in preparation for a downward transition (see page 14), but, instead of making the transition, increase the leg aids so that the horse is encouraged to continue in trot. Maintain the contact and hold the horse in this slower trot for approximately ten strides (fig. 4). You should have the feeling that the horse is

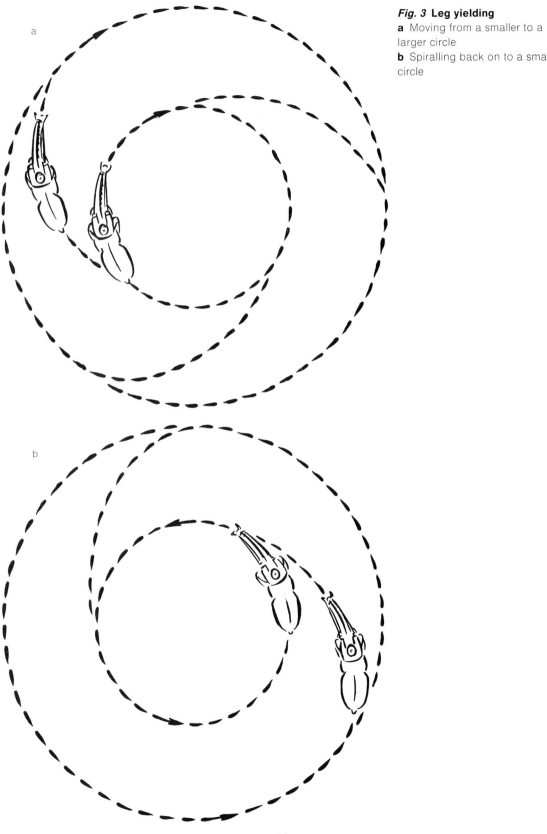

Fig. 3 Leg yielding
a Moving from a smaller to a larger circle
b Spiralling back on to a smaller circle

stepping under his body and raising the forehand, and you should hold this with your seat and legs.

This exercise is best done in rising trot, so that the horse is not encouraged to hollow his back in an attempt to avoid stepping under his body with his hindlegs. When executed correctly, it allows the forehand to remain supple and light. This alleviates the problem of your having to pull on the reins in an attempt to condense the horse's forward movement, forcing him into an artificial outline with a hollow back, which makes it impossible for him to use his hindquarters in the correct way.

After ten strides, ask the horse to go forward again by lightening the contact and closing your legs around his sides. The horse's contained energy should propel him forward, with the strides becoming bigger and longer **(fig. 5)**. If the exercise is executed correctly, the horse will lower his haunches and drive himself forward as his hindlegs become more engaged.

Once the horse has sufficient development, you will have the feeling that the abdominal muscles are supporting and lifting the forehand. The neck will have a slight upward curve from the base through to the poll, which will be the highest point. When the horse becomes more dextrous as the muscle development increases, you will find that you can control the impulsion much more by the use of your seat, upper body and legs. This is because the horse's quarters and hindlegs will be in control of the energy, keeping the forehand light and easy to control, as he will not be leaning on the rein as a means of support.

The same exercise can be used in canter **(fig. 6)**. With time and patience, and by building up the degree of difficulty of the collection and extension, the horse will eventually be able to make a transition from a gallop to a condensed canter within a few strides.

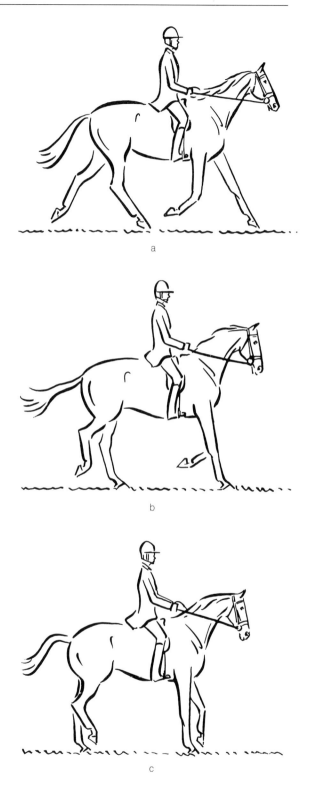

a

b

c

Fig. 4 Decreasing the length of stride in trot. Think of slowing the trot as if in preparation for a downward transition

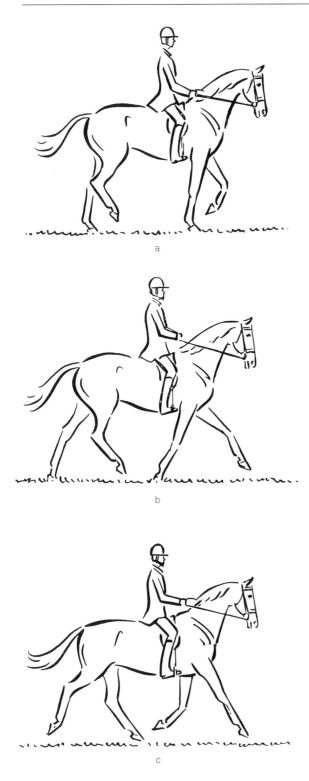

a

b

c

Fig. 5 Increasing the length of stride in trot. After ten strides, the horse should be asked to go forward again

When the horse has become established in this exercise on flat, level ground, he can progress to practising both uphill and downhill. Keep the hills relatively gradual until the horse has developed sufficient balance and control, and copes with the exercise easily. When asking the horse to lengthen his stride on a hill, never throw your weight forward in an attempt to make him do this. All that will happen is that the weight will be transferred to the forehand, so that, when moving uphill, the horse will pull himself along on the forehand, and, when moving downhill, all the weight will be taken on the forehand and forelegs. Instead, use your legs to create more impulsion. This will encourage the horse to step under his body with his hindlegs, and, when he is allowed to go forward, the steps will become longer and cover more ground. This exercise must not be executed on very steep downhill areas because enormous stress will be put on the forelegs, so if a course has a very steep downhill section, do not go fast but try to keep the horse in balance and off the forehand.

When collecting or shortening the canter downhill, sit up and close your legs around the horse. The contact must be kept consistent to help the horse to find his balance, but, if the horse leans on the rein, he will drop on to his forehand and lose his balance. If this happens, bring your shoulders up and back, use a stronger lower leg, and carry out a series of half-halts to encourage the horse to stop leaning, and to regain an elastic contact instead of a wooden one. The horse must learn to regulate the amount of forward movement by using his hindquarters, not only to create the impulsion but also to control it, thus allowing the forehand to remain light and supple. When you wish to slow the canter, 'thinking slower' will slow down the horse, and, as long as you remain in balance with a strong lower leg

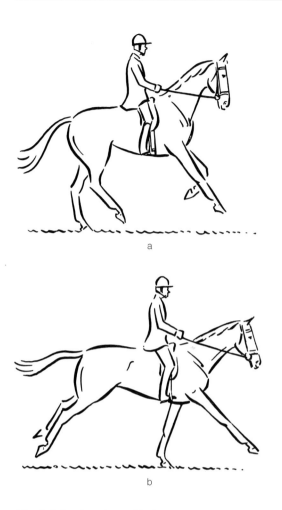

a

b

Fig. 6 Adjusting the stride in canter
a Decreasing the stride length: the horse uses his hindquarters to slow himself down and the hindlegs begin to take smaller steps
b Increasing the stride length: the hindlegs become more active and propel the horse forward

and your shoulders up, it will be possible to maintain the impulsion even though the canter is fairly slow.

When lengthening or shortening the canter while moving uphill, you must keep a stronger than normal lower leg. Remember that the natural tendency is for the horse to slow down when travelling uphill, so if you wish to collect the canter, be sure to keep in balance without getting behind the movement, and use enough lower leg to maintain the impulsion. This is especially important if there is a jump or combination to be negotiated at the top of the hill.

Contained impulsion or energy

Contained impulsion or energy is an expression that is frequently used regarding the approach to obstacles such as coffins, sunken roads, bounces, combinations or fences requiring accurate, controlled jumping.

When riding from fence to fence across country, the horse's outline is usually long and the stride covers a lot of ground. This is adequate if the only obstacles to be jumped are sloping birch fences, but if there is a combination where the distances and terrain require shorter strides and athletic jumping, the stride and outline associated with a galloping horse will be too long. By slowing down the speed within the pace and shortening the stride length, it is possible to arrive at the take-off point with the correct balance, speed and stride length with which to jump the fences successfully. Remember, however, that the slower the canter, the harder it is for the horse, as he has to bend his hind joints to a greater degree to avoid breaking into trot, dropping his weight on the forehand, and losing his rhythm, balance and concentration.

When you ask the horse to slow down, you must help him to establish a shorter, more collected stride without breaking the rhythm. He must also keep a rounded outline. A high, short head and neck carriage combines with a hollow back (see **fig. 2** on page 15), and this will stop the hindlegs from stepping under the body and prevent the horse from containing the energy necessary for jumping the fence,

21

particularly if it is a combination. Instead of pulling on the reins to slow down, lift your shoulders and use your back and legs so that the horse's hindlegs actually slow down and take shorter, more active steps. By sitting up in this way and keeping a firm but elastic contact, you can contain the created energy until it is ready to be released, either by the horse jumping the combination, coping with the terrain or in being allowed to go forward into a longer outline and stride.

Young horses can only hold a more collected and engaged stride and outline for a few seconds. This is because they have not reached a stage of training or muscle development that allows the joints of the hindlegs to bend to a greater degree in order to achieve shorter and more engaged steps. The majority of their weight is still over the forehand, but, with correct training as outlined on pages 17–19, it is possible to develop the horse so that in a matter of strides he is able to go from a gallop to a collected canter, in which the energy is contained in the hindquarters.

Whenever impulsion is being produced, it is important that the forehand remains light, with the horse stepping underneath his body and lifting the forehand. This is especially important when jumping fences with a downhill approach. Unless the forehand is kept light, the horse will find it difficult on take-off to raise his wither, shoulder, head and neck in order to become sufficiently airborne to jump the fence. When the rider constantly fights the horse for control, it is likely to produce a hollow and resistant horse; he will not only be hollow in front of the saddle, blocking the wither and the shoulder on take-off, but will also be hollow in his back, preventing the engagement of the hindlegs and resulting in a lack of impulsion, power and thrust. As the horse cannot operate in this unnatural way, a mistake will be made at the fence, resulting in a loss of confidence for the horse and a reduced trust in his rider.

The horse is not capable of true collection and lightness of the forehand until he has sufficient muscular development to cope with moving weight from the forehand to the hindquarters. If he is to compete at national level and above, however, he must be trained so that he is able to shorten and lengthen his outline and stride when asked while remaining in self-carriage. He must be able to distribute his weight in such a way that he remains in balance, without having to lean on the rein as a means of support.

Combination fences such as coffins, sunken roads and bounces require athletic jumping. An approach in gallop is therefore not suitable, because the horse's outline and strides are too long, the speed is too fast, and the balance is insufficient, so that the horse will be carrying too much weight on the forehand. A more collected outline is ideal because the stride is shorter and more suitable for the distances in the combination, the horse can cope with the terrain more efficiently, the hindlegs will be more engaged with the energy contained until it is needed, the forehand will be lighter (and therefore easier for the horse to raise on take-off), and the balance and speed will be more appropriate for the oncoming combination.

If the speed is too fast, the horse may over-jump any part of the combination. This will result in a loss of balance and a refusal, run out or even a fall. If the speed is too slow, the horse may drop behind the bridle or your leg, so that, when you expect the horse to produce the power and thrust necessary to jump, cope with the ground or go forward with a longer, more powerful stride, he will not be able to achieve this as he will have lost the impulsion or energy.

Establishing a rhythmical canter

A series of canter poles can be used to help the horse to maintain a canter stride of even length. Start with a single pole, and canter to it several times until the pole is negotiated within the canter stride. The horse should not jump the pole, break the rhythm of the canter, or increase or decrease speed. Do not tip yourself forward in anticipation, or try to 'place' the horse at the pole – in time, it will be possible to canter down to the pole accurately every time.

A second pole can then be added approximately 3 metres (10 ft) from the first. Canter to both poles until the horse is able to keep the same rhythm and balance all the time, after which a third pole can be added. The distance between the poles can be shortened or lengthened according to your horse's stride and what you are trying to achieve. Being accurate in your approach to the canter poles will help you to ride to a fence more accurately.

Riding in the cross-country position

When the above exercise is performed with shorter stirrups, the same principle applies, in that you must never pull on the reins to condense the stride. Instead, the seat, upper body and legs are used in conjunction with a firm contact between your hands and the horse's mouth (this contact should have the same flexibility as a strong piece of elastic). The rein contact should never become fixed, as the horse will simply hollow against the restriction so that the hindlegs trail instead of being engaged. Any half-halt should be made within the rhythm of the pace, so that the steps may be condensed or shortened

without the horse resisting. As has been discussed on page 21, the key to cross-country riding is the ability to create or store energy which can then be used at any time for jumping or coping with the terrain. If this energy is allowed to diminish, the horse will be unable to perform his tasks. It is therefore of vital importance to ensure that he has the correct training and is sufficiently developed.

POINTS TO REMEMBER

- The stage of training and development must be equal to the level of competition.
- The horse must not be forced with a restrictive hand into a slower speed.
- The forehand must remain raised and light.
- The quarters must control the speed.
- The rider must keep using the legs so that the energy and impulsion are maintained by the horse's 'engine' (the quarters).
- Any alteration within the pace must be made gradually, and within the rhythm, so that the horse learns to increase and decrease the speed and length of his stride while maintaining a correct and supple outline, good balance and no interruptions to the rhythm. Remember that a slower canter demands a stronger leg aid to prevent the horse from falling into trot.

Riding on differing terrain

The most important factor here is that you must try to remain in balance with the horse at all times, and never become a hindrance. With your stirrups at cross-country length, practise keeping your position in balance at all paces on flat ground. Until you are capable of this, you will always hinder the horse instead of helping him when riding up or down hills, or on awkward ground such as ridge and furrow.

Riding uphill

The natural inclination is for you to get behind the movement and for the horse to slow down **(2)**, but, by securing a correct lower-leg position, you should be able to bring your body slightly forward from the knee upward. Your lower legs must remain in the correct position, as, if they slip back, you will become unbalanced and have to hold on to the mane in order to stop yourself from slipping backward. Practise in walk at first, then in trot and then in canter.

The horse needs to lower and lengthen his neck when travelling uphill, so you must allow for this with the rein – but without dropping the contact – by extend-

2 This rider is behind the movement and the horse is hollowing against her weight

3 Here the rider's lower legs have slipped back, causing loss of balance. In this position she cannot use her legs to maintain the impulsion, and is restricting the horse's head and neck movement by leaning on his withers for balance

ing your arms towards his mouth. If you lose your balance, you may have to rest your hands on the horse's withers, making the contact fixed and unpleasant for him because it restricts his head and neck movement (3). As well as concentrating on the balance, you must encourage the horse to move in a straight line. If you allow him to drift when going uphill, it will be difficult to take a certain line up a hill to a fence and arrive at the correct point.

Working the horse up hills is excellent for developing muscles and fitness, but it is quite stressful, especially in the early stages, so do not do too much in one session. Try to keep your weight off the horse's back when trotting uphill. In canter, it is important to keep the horse in a rhythm, and under control, rather than letting him gallop in an undisciplined way (4) and (5).

Riding downhill

It is essential for the cross-country horse to learn to maintain the correct pace, impulsion, speed and balance when moving downhill. The horse's weight naturally appears to drop on to the forehand, but course builders often construct fences at the bottom of hills, so this weight needs to be transferred further back. If the

4 (*Top left*) The young horse finds it much easier to bound up the hill rather than canter up

5 (*Bottom left*) The older horse cantering up the hill. She is able to remain in balance and the rider is not interfering with her, but the rider's lower legs and hips could be a little further forward to allow the hands forward a little more, so that she may have a shorter rein. Both horse and rider are looking in the direction in which they are going

weight is not kept off the forehand, the horse's jumping will be very hit-and-miss. He will also drift rather than travelling in a straight line when his balance is insecure, and, unless this is corrected, he will reach the take-off point to a fence out of balance, which could result in a refusal or a fall.

Begin by walking the horse downhill. Even at this pace, he will find it very difficult at first to keep the rhythm or the balance. Allow your legs to go forward to act as a balancing point, and keep your seat lightly in the saddle, resisting the temptation to lean back and sit heavily. If this happens, the horse will hollow his back against you, limiting the use of his hindlegs to control himself. Be sure that the horse walks slowly, step by step, so that the pace does not gain momentum and speed **(6)**. It will be difficult for him to remain in a straight line initially, but,

6 This horse has not tried to walk down the hill step by step – instead, she has just bucked! This is a sign that she is not yet in control of her body

7 The older horse walking quietly down the hill. By taking it step by step, she is able to remain in balance. The rider's otherwise good position is marred by having collapsed her right hip to look down the horse's shoulder

with time and as his confidence grows, it will become possible at all paces **(7)**.

As the horse increases in confidence and balance, you can begin to practise negotiating hills in canter. Young horses will obviously not have the development to cope in canter down steep hills, but if you have carried out the basic training prog-

ramme correctly on the flat, as already outlined, it will be possible to negotiate gradual declines in canter with the horse keeping the majority of his weight on his quarters to control the forward momentum **(8–10)**.

As his development and strength increase with training, a much greater degree of collection and control will be possible in canter. In time, the horse will be able to cope with steeper slopes, and negotiating complex obstacles, even with a downhill take-off, will be relatively straightforward.

8 The rider is doing her best to contain this horse. She has a good lower-leg position and has kept her shoulders up. The horse's outline is a little hollow and could be rounder

9 The horse looks much rounder here. The rider has let her shoulders slip forward a little, and her hands look a little set on the horse's neck

10 The horse's outline and stride are beginning to get very long. The rider is trying to rectify the fault by sitting up and holding the horse together, but it is probably too late to engage him as he has already become hollow and on his forehand

Uneven ground

Successful cross-country riding is based on the maintenance of a good, even rhythm throughout the whole course, but uneven ground such as ridge and furrow makes it difficult to maintain this rhythm. A young horse can become very perturbed if the terrain or state of the ground changes, because his balance is not secure enough to cope with it, but, as he gains experience and becomes more balanced and better developed, he will find it easier to deal with uneven ground. To help him gain confidence, most of his training should be carried out on good ground, to give him the security needed to proceed up the training ladder.

If a young horse suddenly encounters some uneven ground, it will usually throw him off balance and affect his rhythm, resulting in loss of impulsion and weight falling on his forehand, where he feels that your rein contact will support him. Once again, the basic training exercises already outlined are instrumental in producing a horse capable of adjusting his length of stride and speed to suit the changes in the ground, resulting in better balance. If you look after the impulsion, the speed and especially the balance during training, the horse will be well-prepared and will have the best possible chance of maintaining a rhythm over uneven ground.

False ground

The ground is said to be false when it changes very suddenly, often with no outward signs. False ground may be caused by an underground pipeline, a natural spring, rabbit warrens or molehills, filled-in streams or ponds, holes, or subsiding or waterlogged land. It can result in severe muscle, tendon or ligament strain, as, if the horse puts his foot to ground which gives way, he has to extend the leg further than expected, over-exerting the body structures and causing strain. Correct training and fitness will enable the muscles to contract and relax to the maximum of their ability, so that, if the horse gallops into false ground, he can re-balance himself very quickly, lessening the chance of injury.

As the horse finds security from good, even ground, he will try to negotiate false ground as economically as possible, but this can only happen if the false ground covers a small area. If it continues for a greater distance, he will be able to adapt his balance, speed and impulsion to suit the ground, as long as he was well-balanced before he hits it. From this point, you must let the horse find his own way, by sitting quietly and in balance, and keeping contact with the rein to minimize the likelihood of excessive weight dropping on to the forehand and forelegs.

Hunting

Although hunting may not be everyone's choice, it can be a useful way of teaching the young horse to go across country and to cope with all terrains and different types of going. He will also learn to pick his way over the country, to find his way through wooded areas and to be brave over natural fences and hazards. Hunting has the additional benefit of helping the young horse to gain confidence in the company of other horses, and to be patient and learn good manners. Hunting can also be used to re-build the confidence of an older horse which has become unsure due to a fall, injury or bad riding.

SUMMARY

- Training on the flat is of great benefit to the cross-country horse, as it helps him to carry himself and you with the maximum of ease and the minimum of effort. The correctly trained and developed horse will suffer less of the wear and tear associated with cross country, which will prolong and enhance his competitive career.
- The balance learned during this early training is the basis of good cross-country riding, enabling the horse to negotiate differing terrain and to jump using his energy economically. This means that you can communicate more effectively with him in terms of his direction, pace and rhythm, and can present him at each fence with all the ingredients necessary to produce a good jump.
- Transitions are an excellent way of teaching balance. Be specific and clear with your aids, and always allow plenty of time to prepare the horse for the next movement.
- When the horse is confident with exercises on level ground, progress to practising both uphill and downhill, to improve the horse's balance and prepare him for the fences that he will encounter on hills on a course. Hill work is excellent for fitness and development, but remember that it can be quite stressful in the early stages.
- Contained impulsion is created by slowing the speed and shortening the stride length to establish a more collected stride. This is achieved not by pulling on the reins, but by lifting your shoulders and using your back and legs so that the horse's hindlegs actually slow down and take shorter, more active steps. The energy created can be contained until it is ready to be released in jumping, coping with the terrain or going forward into a longer stride.
- Remember that perfection takes time to achieve. Aim to progress a little at a time, and be careful not to confuse or bore the horse by trying to teach him too much at once.

2
EARLY JUMP TRAINING

The horse can begin to learn about jumping as soon as he is going quietly in walk and trot, as the early stages are not really about actual jumping, but learning to cross over poles and small natural hazards.

Loose schooling

Loose schooling is an ideal introduction to jumping for the young horse, as he can concentrate entirely on the task in hand, without the encumbrance of your weight. It is an excellent way of teaching the basic technique. Building a jumping lane is very simple. All that is required is a well-fenced area with a good non-slip surface and a perimeter fence high enough to prevent the horse from jumping out. Show-jumping wings and poles can be used to make a lane, which should be approximately 4 metres (12 ft) wide, using the permanent fence on the long side of the arena as one side of the lane (fig. 7).

First of all, let the horse go down the lane once or twice, in both directions, using your voice to encourage him. (A lunge whip may also be used if necessary to encourage him forward and to prevent him from turning round.) Then lay a pole on the ground across the lane, and let the horse come down to it from both directions. Next, a cross pole can replace the pole on the ground, with the horse again allowed to approach from both directions. At this stage it does not matter whether the horse trots or canters, as long as he has sufficient impulsion and is not losing his balance on the corners before the fence. The arc of the jump may not yet be correct, but this will soon improve with practice as the horse learns to control his body and legs. Do not over-do the jumping at first, or the horse will become bored and stale. The young horse tires very quickly, and if he is tired he will make mistakes.

To help the horse to arrive at the correct take-off point, a placing pole can be introduced 2·3 to 2·7 metres ($7\frac{1}{2}$ to 9 ft) from the cross pole (fig. 8). This is an ideal distance from trot, but may encourage the horse to jump the pole and cross pole all in one if approached in canter. A pole placed at 5.5 to 6 metres (18 to 20 ft) will allow the horse to take one stride between the pole and the cross pole in canter. When loose jumping without a placing pole, ensure that you have a good ground line, which will help the horse to come to a good take-off point.

A second fence can then be added at a distance of 5.5 to 6 metres (18 to 20 ft) from the cross pole. At first, a pole on the ground will suffice, but, once the horse is confident over a cross pole, the second fence can be changed to an upright and then an ascending spread.

Fig. 7 Show-jumping wings and
poles can be used to build a
jumping lane in an enclosed area

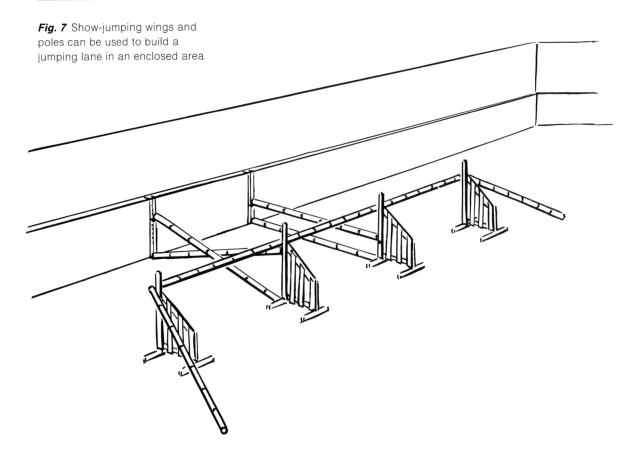

Fig. 8 Introducing a placing pole
before a cross pole. The distance
between the two can be adjusted,
depending on the horse's length
of stride and stage of training

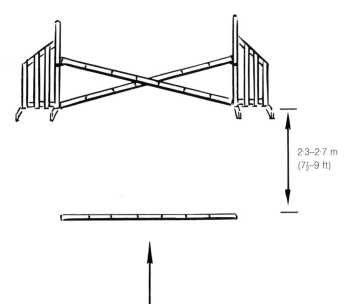

2·3–2·7 m
(7½–9 ft)

Always remember to keep the exercises simple and fun, and well within the horse's capabilities. If you have a problem where the horse loses confidence, you must regain that confidence before he is taken back to his stable, so, if the horse does something well, stop there rather than trying something new, and build up the exercise over a matter of time.

Jumping when ridden

Your horse must first become familiar with poles on the ground. These can be introduced either in the schooling area, or out on a ride, where the horse can be asked to walk or trot over broken branches or other natural objects.

Poles in walk

In the schooling area, single poles placed at random are an ideal beginning. Once the horse has mastered these, he can progress to a series of poles. If approaching in walk, set out three to five poles with 1 metre (3 ft) between each **(fig. 9)**, or set them out at 2 metre (6 ft) distances. The first arrangement requires the horse to walk over the poles at every step; the latter requires him to step over the poles every stride. The latter method is easier initially, as it gives the horse more room between the poles, and it is easier for him to understand what is being asked of him.

The horse must not rush or jump the poles, but should come down to them quietly and calmly, keeping the walk rhythmical and the outline soft and free from tension. If he arrives at the first pole and stops dead, encourage him to walk forward by using your legs and voice, with the command 'walk on'. A schooling whip used just behind the lower leg will reinforce your leg aid. If he still refuses to go forward, go back to a single pole, then add

Fig. 9 Poles in walk. Set out the poles with 1 m (3 ft) between each

another one 3 to 4 metres (10 to 12 ft) from the first. Once he is confident with these, a third pole may be added at the same distance, and then the distance gradually closed down to 2 metres (6 ft). If the horse is uncertain or anxious in any way, the poles can be walked over every day until he accepts them as part of his everyday life.

Trotting poles

Introduce trotting poles in the same way that you started with the walking poles, placing them at random around the school. Try to judge the placing of the feet in relation to the poles so that the horse trots over the poles within his stride, without having to break the rhythm in order to negotiate them. As with the walk, there must be no anxiety, tension or rushing, but a quiet approach with the horse concentrating on the job in hand. If he insists on rushing, approach each pole from a circle, so that, being on a continual curve, he does not have a chance to rush off.

To introduce a line of trotting poles, place three or more poles spaced at intervals of 1·3 metres (4½ ft), or at 2·7 metres (9 ft). The first arrangement requires the horse to negotiate the poles at every stride; the latter requires him to trot over a pole every other stride. It is unwise to use only two poles at the shorter distance, as the horse may be encouraged to jump them. If your horse is a little uncertain, use the wider distance initially, and introduce one extra pole at a time. The distances may need shortening or lengthening depending on the horse's stride length: as a guide, he should put his feet on the ground at an equal distance from each pole (fig. 10).

When using trotting poles, it is helpful to have someone on the ground to alter the distances as and when necessary. Remember that there should be no panicking, anxiety or rushing, and, if the horse is unsure, practise the poles every day until he becomes confident and remains relaxed. It is important to keep the horse straight and to bring him to the middle of the poles at the correct place, so that he does not have to break the stride to trot over the first one.

Fig. 10 Trotting poles. Adjust the distance between them so that the horse trots over them evenly

Introducing the first fence

Once your horse has mastered these poles, a jump can be introduced. Put out a pair of wings and lay some poles down by the side, and allow the horse to pass between the wings before a jump is introduced. Place another pole approximately 2·3 to 2·6 metres (7½ to 9 ft) in front of and parallel to the wings. Trot the horse over the pole and between the wings. Place another pole on the ground between the wings, and trot over the two poles (fig. 11).

If the horse is going forward confidently, introduce a small cross pole, about 30 centimetres (1 ft) high; a cross pole will help him to come to the middle of the fence, as a horse will usually jump a fence at the smallest part (see fig. 8 on page 33). Leave the placing pole at the same distance as before to help the horse arrive at the correct take-off position for the cross pole. Be sure to keep him straight, and bring him to the middle of the placing pole so that he is lined up for the middle of the cross pole.

At first the jump will be quite laboured, but be sure to allow the horse enough rein so that he can stretch his head and neck over the cross pole. A young horse usually jumps in a very deliberate way, so you must remain in balance with secure lower legs, or you may hinder him. If the horse backs off the cross pole, you must be quick to create more impulsion with your legs, or he will have to haul himself over the jump, or, if the impulsion dies altogether, he may refuse or fall through it.

On landing, ride away in a straight line, preferably in canter so that the horse learns to go forward instead of landing in a heap. This is especially important when a second fence is added. Jumping the cross pole three to four times from each direction is sufficient for the first lesson, as a tired horse will make mistakes and he must go back to his stable having enjoyed himself. After two or three lessons the horse should be gaining control of his body and his legs.

If at any time things go wrong, go back to poles on the ground and then build up to the cross pole again gradually. Ideally, at this stage, the horse should be balanced and straight when approaching the pole, with the trot going forward. On reaching the pole, he should step over it so that, when he comes to taking off for the cross

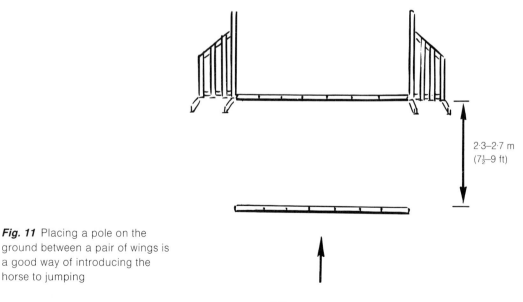

2·3–2·7 m
(7½–9 ft)

Fig. 11 Placing a pole on the ground between a pair of wings is a good way of introducing the horse to jumping

pole, both hindlegs are between the placing pole and the cross pole, giving him a balanced take-off platform. If the horse dives at the fence and takes off when his hindlegs are still on the approach side of the placing pole, the jump will be flat and strung out. It is acceptable for the horse to jump the placing pole, provided that his hindlegs are on the side closest to the cross pole before he takes off over it. If, however, the horse jumps the placing pole by diving at it, he will be thrown off balance and on his forehand when taking off for the cross pole. If he jumps the placing and cross poles together, either the approach was too fast, or the placing pole was too close to the cross pole, in which case the distance should be opened up a little.

A series of trot poles can now be used in front of the cross pole, with the distance from the last pole to the cross pole being approximately 2·3 to 2·7 metres (7½ to 9 ft)

depending on the length of your horse's stride (fig. 12). Be sure that your horse is familiar with the trot poles before introducing them in front of the cross pole. Always use three or more poles, as two will encourage the horse to jump them, and check that the distance is suitable for that particular horse. The horse must be kept balanced, rhythmical and going forward over the trot poles, or he will find the cross pole difficult. This exercise should be a natural progression from trotting over the poles on their own.

Once again, the cross pole encourages the horse to come to the middle of the fence. The higher the cross pole, the more the horse has to use his shoulders, forearms and forelegs to avoid hitting the fence, so do not make the cross too severe for the younger horse. The placing pole encourages the horse to come to a closer take-off point and, by bringing the hindlegs underneath the body, enables the

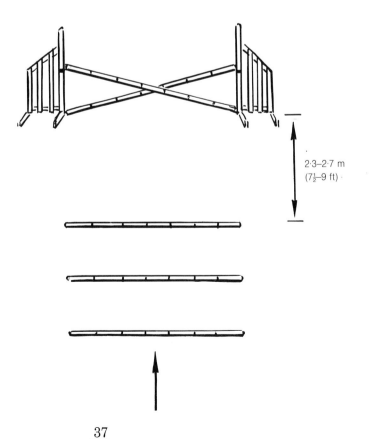

2·3–2·7 m
(7½–9 ft)

Fig. 12 A series of trot poles to a cross pole

forehand to remain light and the abdominal muscles to help lift the forehand up and over the fence. The trotting poles encourage the horse to maintain an even rhythm and balance on the last few strides prior to take-off, and also help with a horse which insists on rushing at his fences.

As the horse becomes more developed and confident, the cross pole can be changed to an upright. Do not attempt a parallel until the horse is capable of engaging his hindquarters, compressing the impulsion and lightening his forehand on take-off. If you try to jump a parallel from trot with a horse who jumps off his forehand, he will be able to make the

height but not the spread, so the result will be a bad experience and a loss of confidence for the horse.

Introducing a second fence

Once the horse has mastered a single fence and is able to remain in balance on the landing side, a second fence can be introduced. Start by placing another pair of wings 5·4 to 6·3 metres (18 to 21 ft) beyond the first cross pole. Let the horse go down between them before any poles are added. Next, place a pole on the ground between the wings, as for a single fence. Approach the placing pole to the cross pole in trot, as

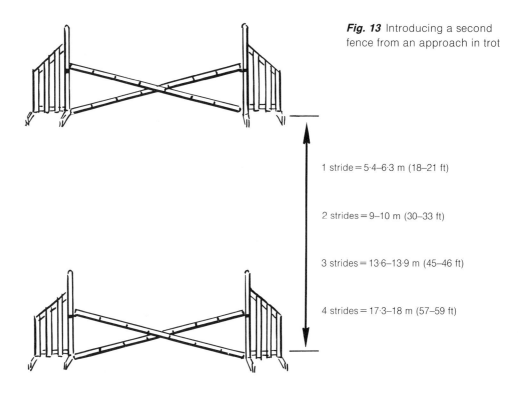

Fig. 13 Introducing a second fence from an approach in trot

1 stride = 5·4–6·3 m (18–21 ft)

2 strides = 9–10 m (30–33 ft)

3 strides = 13·6–13·9 m (45–46 ft)

4 strides = 17·3–18 m (57–59 ft)

before, and then keep the horse straight until he has crossed over the second pole.

At this stage the horse is bound to waver a little, so it is your job to help to keep him straight and balanced by ensuring that your own position does not become unbalanced. If a young horse makes big, awkward jumps, it can be a wise precaution to fit a neck strap to hold on to, so that you do not catch him in the mouth. If the horse lands in trot, keep your legs on a little more the next time to encourage him to land in canter. Once the horse is able to negotiate the second pole with ease, a small cross pole can replace the pole **(fig. 13)**. Having negotiated both fences, ride away in a balanced manner. If the horse finds the distance between the two fences a little long or short, adjust the distance accordingly.

Once the horse has mastered this exercise, the second fence can be altered to a two-strided distance. 9 to 10 metres (30 to 33 ft) is usually ideal, but, if you are not sure, place a pole on the ground initially and see whether the horse takes two comfortable strides. If he stretches to reach the pole, the distance is too long, or the impulsion has faded after the first fence; if he only had just enough room to put in the two strides, the distance is too short, or the horse quickened after the first fence. With a little practice, you will be able to judge the correct distance between the two fences.

Once the horse is confident with the two-strided fence, the distance can be altered again so that he learns to take three and four strides in canter between the two fences. For three strides, place the second fence approximately 13·7 metres (45 ft) from the first fence. For four strides, the distance between the two will be approximately 17·3 metres (57 ft). If you are unsure of the distance, use a pole on the ground first as described above.

Remember that the young horse can

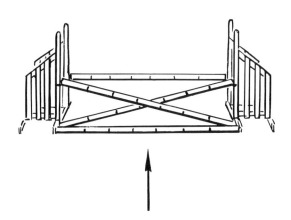

Fig. 14 A small ascending spread makes an inviting fence

wobble quite considerably between his fences, so fix your eye on the centre of the second fence. Concentrating on the middle of the pole in this way will help you to keep the horse straight during the non-jumping strides. When the horse is confident over the two fences, the second fence can have a back rail added to make it into a small ascending spread **(fig. 14)**. Keep the back rail to a height of 45 centimetres (18 ins) so that, if the horse does make a mistake, it will be of little consequence. A small filler or barrels can be put under the second fence as an introduction to fillers, but remove the back rail in case the horse jumps very high but not wide enough. When out on a hack, small logs, hedges, banks, ditches and posts and rails can be introduced, as long as they are small and well within the horse's capabilities. It is wise to be accompanied by an older, more experienced horse in case the young horse needs a lead over an obstacle.

At this early stage, an approach in trot is usually favoured. It is your duty to present the horse at the fence with the best possible chance of jumping it, so you must make a straight approach with the horse attentive, in balance and with sufficient impulsion. As young horses like to weigh up the situation, it is important to approach with increasing impulsion so that, if the horse backs off a little, there will still be enough energy from which to jump. Always reward your horse and jump the fence two or three times in both directions so that he gains confidence. Make sure that, on landing, you ride away from the fence and help the horse to regain his balance as quickly as possible. This is relevant for future cross-country training, when it will be just as important to land in balance as it is to take off in balance. If everything goes to pieces on the landing side, it will be difficult to string together a series of fences.

Always keep the jumping interesting by introducing different types of fences, but be certain that you never ask the horse to do too much, and that you have planned the approach correctly. A combination of fences in the school and those encountered while out riding is an ideal situation. Two or three small jumps can be included in the daily programme, or, if it is more practical, allocate one or two of your training periods per week to jumping.

Jumping from canter

At this stage the horse has jumped from canter, but only as a result of landing in canter from the previous fence. The young horse's canter is usually long, rather unbalanced and difficult to alter, making an accurate approach to a fence quite difficult, but the use of canter poles, as explained on page 23, can help the horse to establish the rhythmic, balanced canter required for jumping. Before approaching fences in canter, the horse must be able to canter in a straight line and on a 20 metre

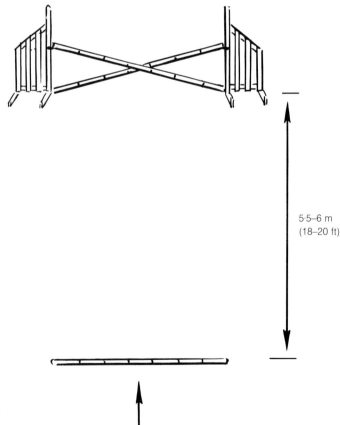

5·5–6 m
(18–20 ft)

Fig. 15 Introducing a canter pole before a cross pole

(66 ft) circle without losing the balance, rhythm or outline, and the rider must be able to make minor adjustments to the canter steps.

Teaching the horse to approach in canter can once again be achieved with the help of poles. Practise trotting to a pole placed at random on the ground. On reaching the pole, close your legs around the horse and pick up canter. Once this is mastered, place the pole approximately 5·5 to 6 metres (18 to 20 ft) in front of a cross pole **(fig. 15)**. Approach the pole in trot as before, and then pick up canter at the pole and canter the one stride to the fence, so that the horse arrives at the correct take-off point. If you fail to pick up canter at the pole, just trot down to the fence, and the horse will soon realize what is required.

Once this exercise has been mastered, practise cantering to poles at random on the ground, and then progress again to placing the pole at the same distance as before in front of the fence. If you misjudge the poles, the horse will either have to lengthen his outline or stride, or shorten or even break his stride, causing his balance to be affected. If this theory is related to approaching a fence, it soon becomes obvious how it affects the quality of the take-off, and subsequently the jump. With practice, however, you will be able to canter accurately every time to the pole in front of the fence – so that the pole is incorporated within the canter stride – and then to sit still during the last stride before take-off.

A horse whose canter stride is very long will make up too much ground over the pole, leaving too little room for the final stride so that his take-off point is too close to the fence. As he is then likely to hit the fence, he will soon learn to condense the stride unless he likes hitting himself. He will also start to control his strides, so that he learns to become more accurate at the take-off point. The longer the canter stride, the larger the margin for error at the take-off point, while the shorter the canter stride, the smaller is the margin for error. This is why ponies or small, neat horses appear to be more accurate to a fence than larger horses.

When you have mastered cantering down to the poles and the rhythm and balance are becoming consistent, the quality of the canter will improve, which is the basis of all successful jumping. Progress from the poles to cantering down to a small cross pole with a good ground line, which will help you and the horse to arrive accurately at the fence.

Always concentrate on the quality of the canter so that the jumping is easy for the horse. If he becomes excited every time he sees a fence, keep cantering past it until he learns not to become excited at the prospect of jumping. Excitement causes tension, which leads to stress and strain, so the horse should understand that jumping is a part of his training and not an excuse for high spirits. Once he has become established over his fences in the schooling area, natural obstacles can be added to the list of fences jumped in canter. When the horse has mastered all the little fences and is jumping them in good style, he can progress to jumping a small, simple course, and gradually the fences can be raised and widened. When first jumping a course, keep the fences below 1 metre (3 ft) until the horse is capable of maintaining a good, rhythmical, balanced canter throughout the whole course. As the horse will be jumping from canter instead of trot, as described on page 32, the distances between the fences may need altering. If you intend to jump the horse at a show for practice, he must be familiar with the distances that the course builders will use. For example:

- a one-strided double measures 7 to 8 metres (24 to 28 ft)

- a two-strided double measures 10·5 to 11·5 metres (34 to 38 ft)
- a related distance with three non-jumping strides measures 13·5 to 14·5 metres (45 to 48 ft)
- a related distance with four non-jumping strides measures 18 metres (59 ft)

These are approximate distances, and may be lengthened or shortened by the course builder. This is why it is so important to teach the horse to shorten and lengthen his stride in canter and to be accurate to the fence. If he cannot do this, he may be unable to make up the distance between the fences if he has not covered enough ground over the first fence, especially if the take-off point was too far away.

In show jumping, the distances are based on the horse's stride covering 3·6 metres (12 ft) with another 1·8 metres (6 ft) being covered for both the take-off and landing. This works well if your horse covers the 1·8 metres (6 ft) allocated for

landing, but if he only covers 1·2 metres (4 ft) he will either have to produce a 4·3 metre (14 ft) stride or take off 2·4 metres (8 ft) from the next fence **(fig. 16)**. If in addition the course builder has made the distance between the two fences rather long, you may have considerable problems if you misjudge the approach to the first fence, or if you have not taught your horse to be versatile within his stride.

It soon becomes clear how important it is to have strides of even length when jumping related distances. As an example, an 18 metre (60 ft) distance allows for four 3·6 metre (12 ft) strides with another 3·6 metres (12 ft) for the take-off and landing. If you have jumped over the first fence, landing 1·8 metres (6 ft) from it, and then each of your next two strides are only 3 metres (10 ft) long, your last two strides will have to be 4·3 metres (14 ft) long if you wish to make up the distance and arrive at the correct take-off point **(fig. 17)**. Conversely, when the distances are shortened between the fences, each of the strides must be altered accordingly, or the horse will arrive at the second fence too close for the take-off.

Fig. 16 Correct and incorrect take-off and landing positions

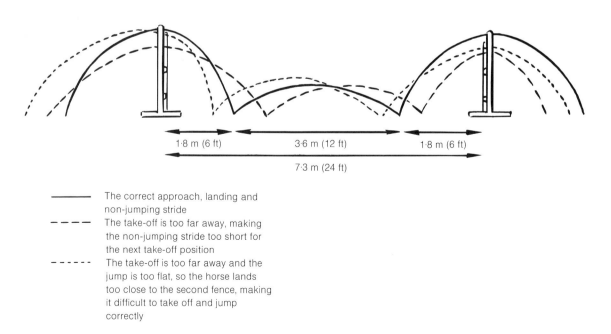

|←—— 1·8 m (6 ft) ——→|←——— 3·6 m (12 ft) ———→|←—— 1·8 m (6 ft) ——→|

|←——————————————— 7·3 m (24 ft) ———————————————→|

—————— The correct approach, landing and non-jumping stride

– – – – The take-off is too far away, making the non-jumping stride too short for the next take-off position

– - – - – The take-off is too far away and the jump is too flat, so the horse lands too close to the second fence, making it difficult to take off and jump correctly

Practise riding down related distances so that you learn to feel when the canter is suitable. It is often a matter of creating a little more impulsion, or keeping the horse a little more together, so that the quality of the canter improves. This is particularly important on a cross-country course when related distances and combinations are sited on undulating terrain. The strides tend to become a little shorter when the horse is going uphill, so a little more lower leg will be required; and when going downhill the steps tend to become a little longer, so you must keep your shoulders up to stop the horse's weight from dropping on to the forehand.

Bounces

A horse 'bounces' between two fences when the distance between them is too small for him to put in a stride, so that he lands and takes off again immediately. When a bounce fence is constructed on a cross-country course on level terrain, the distance between the two elements is

GOLDEN RULES FOR JUMPING AT AN EARLY STAGE

- Keep the fences small, and wide enough to discourage run-outs.
- The ground during the approach and the take-off and landing points must be good, true and not sloping across the width of the fence.
- The siting of the obstacles must enable the horse to make an easy approach.
- The fences should look inviting and solid, not flimsy or spooky.
- Avoid sudden changes of light – for example, jumping in or out of a wood.
- Always keep the jumping fun and interesting – do not overdo it and sicken the horse.
- The distances for this stage of training are only approximate, and can be altered to suit the horse's stride length.

usually 4 to 4·5 metres ($13\frac{1}{2}$ to $14\frac{1}{2}$ ft), but, for the purposes of training the young horse, a bounce of 3 metres (10 ft) can be introduced into the jumping exercises so that he can approach it in trot (**fig. 18**). This can be done once the horse is familiar with approaching, jumping and landing over a variety of fences set at related distances.

Fig. 17 The importance of having strides of even length in a related distance

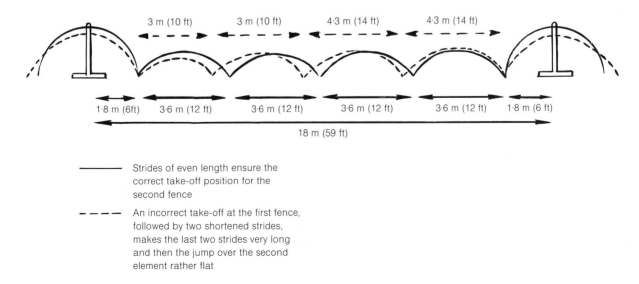

3 m (10 ft)   3 m (10 ft)   4·3 m (14 ft)   4·3 m (14 ft)

1·8 m (6ft)   3·6 m (12 ft)   3·6 m (12 ft)   3·6 m (12 ft)   3·6 m (12 ft)   1·8 m (6 ft)

18 m (59 ft)

——— Strides of even length ensure the correct take-off position for the second fence

– – – – An incorrect take-off at the first fence, followed by two shortened strides, makes the last two strides very long and then the jump over the second element rather flat

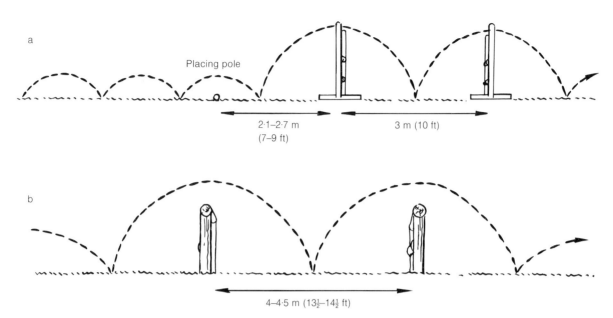

a

Placing pole

2·1–2·7 m
(7–9 ft)

3 m (10 ft)

b

4–4·5 m (13½–14½ ft)

Fig. 18 A bounce fence
a When introducing a bounce fence into the training programme, an approach in trot is advisable. This necessitates a shorter distance between the two fences
b A bounce on a cross-country course has a longer distance, as an approach in a forward-thinking canter is the usual practice

It is advisable to encourage the horse to go forward well in his jumping before introducing a bounce, as, although this involves jumping the obstacles without a stride between the two, the horse must keep going forward. Start by constructing a cross pole, with a placing pole 2·1 to 2·7 metres (7 to 9 ft) in front of it if required. Trot to the placing pole, jump the cross and ride forward and straight on landing and the getaway. Practise this exercise approaching from both directions and riding away with a change of rein each time.

The next stage is to construct a second cross pole approximately 3 metres (10 ft) from the first. Check that the centres of the crosses are aligned to encourage the horse to keep straight. Approach the cross poles as before, with contained impulsion in trot. The horse will jump the first cross, land and immediately jump the second one. Ride forward on landing and praise your horse generously. Practise this a few times so that the horse knows exactly what is expected of him. If the horse struggles to jump the second cross, check that the distance is not too long, and that on the approach the trot is going forward straight and in balance, with enough impulsion. If the energy is not maintained to the first cross pole, the horse will struggle over the second. If he lands too close to the second cross, open up the distance a little. With a backward-thinking or stuffy horse, try cantering until two or three strides before the placing pole so that you can have more energy in the trot. Once the horse is accustomed to the two cross poles, a third can be introduced at the same distance. As before, check that the crosses are aligned. Another good exercise is to replace the second cross pole with a small upright fence, discarding the third cross. Adjust the distance between the two fences to suit your horse's stride.

The next step is to progress to jumping

from canter. Remove the placing pole and move the second part of the bounce to a distance of approximately 3·7 metres (12 ft) **(fig. 19)**. Check the quality of the canter before you approach the bounce. It should feel active, engaged and supple with a true three-time beat, and the horse should be attentive and responsive to your aids. Ride to the middle of the cross pole on a good, even stride, keeping your legs on so that the impulsion is maintained. With your upper body, wait for the horse to take off over the cross pole and then follow through over the second part – do not get in front of the movement by tipping forward with your upper body in anticipation of the take-off. This is a bad habit, as it unbalances and unnerves the horse and puts extra weight on the forehand. By tipping forward like this, you will also unbalance yourself, so that if your horse backed off the fence or veered to the left or right, you would not be in a position to help him.

During the next few jumping sessions, practise jumping bounces, building up to a bounce of two uprights. In order to jump a proper cross-country bounce of 4 to 4·5 metres (13½ to 14½ ft) (see **fig. 18** on page 44), a little more impulsion needs to be introduced into the canter, or, having jumped into the bounce, there will be too much distance and the horse will become confused. Always approach the first element with sufficient impulsion – not so that the horse gains speed on the approach, but so that, on take-off, the compressed or contained impulsion carries him far enough over the first element.

Solving basic problems

Until the horse gains confidence with experience, he is bound to make mistakes when jumping. Many of these problems can be solved by the use of poles, as already described, or by changing the nature of the fence. Listed below are some ways in which to solve two common faults, but if you are experiencing difficulties with which you cannot establish the cause, let alone the cure, it is advisable to seek help from someone whose knowledge you respect.

Losing too much ground between fences

If you find that your horse has too much distance to make up between two fences set at a related distance:

- approach the first fence with a little more impulsion
- ride away on the landing side of the first fence with a stronger leg aid and a little more purpose
- if the horse ignores your leg aid, reinforce it by using the whip behind your lower leg
- shorten the distance between the two fences by approximately 1 metre (3 ft)
- check that the nature of the fence is not too difficult for the horse's stage of training
- take a lead from a more experienced horse

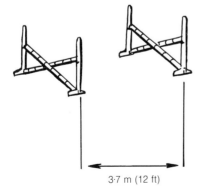

3·7 m (12 ft)

Fig. 19 A training bounce suitable for an approach in canter

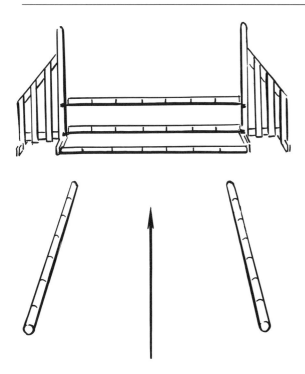

Fig 20 Poles laid at 90° to the wings encourage a straight approach

- open up the distances between the fences by approximately 1 metre (3 ft)
- place a filler under the fences to encourage the horse to back off a little and look at what he is doing

Using poles to aid training

Poles can be used on the ground in a variety of ways:

- to keep the horse straight on the approach and bring him to the middle of the fence
- to help him to arrive at the correct take-off point while remaining in balance
- to encourage a horse which rushes to slow down
- to encourage the horse to jump in better style and to stay straight over the fence
- to help the horse to pick up canter prior to the fence

Making up too much ground between fences

If you find that your horse is over-keen between fences:

- sit very still between the fences
- do not let your upper body tip forward in anticipation of the take-off, as this will encourage the horse to go faster
- try not to throw your upper body too far forward over the fence, as this may cause the horse to lengthen his stride and become unbalanced
- keep your hands forward on the approach and over the fence, and never pull back in an attempt to slow the horse
- approach the first fence from trot a few times until the horse settles
- establish the canter before attempting the jump so that the horse stops anticipating it

Poles placed on the take-off side

- Poles laid at 90° to the wings of the fence during the approach can help to keep a wobbly, green horse straight. The horse almost shies away from the poles, which are placed on each side of him on the approach to form a channel which discourages wavering **(fig. 20)**.
- Some horses jump crookedly, resulting in a poor jump and an unbalanced landing. Poles rested at 90° to the wings, with one end supported on the jump pole and the other end resting on the ground encourage the horse to stay straight during the take-off and jump **(fig. 21)**.
- A good ground line encourages the horse to arrive at the correct take-off point. Bringing the ground line directly underneath the jump pole encourages a close take-off point, so that the horse has to lift his withers, shoulders and forelegs up more quickly in order to

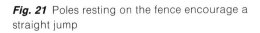

Fig. 21 Poles resting on the fence encourage a straight jump

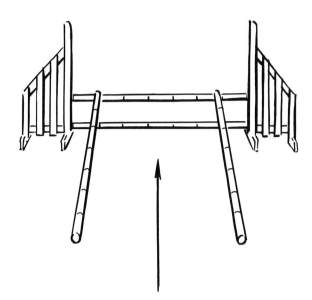

avoid hitting the fence with his fore-arms or lower legs **(fig. 22)**.

Poles placed on the landing side

- A pole placed 3 to 3·5 metres (10 to 12 ft) parallel and beyond the fence on the landing side **(fig. 23)** encourages the horse to:

  (a) jump the fence with a smaller arc so that he lands before negotiating the pole
  (b) lower his head and neck in order to negotiate the pole
  (c) remain in balance after landing
  (d) make up less distance over the fence
  (e) arrive at the correct take-off point for the next fence
  (f) open up his outline during the non-jumping strides
  (g) shorten his outline if he makes up too much ground between fences

- Poles placed at 90° to the wings on the landing side of the fence can help to

Fig. 22 Ground lines
a A good ground line encourages the horse to arrive at the correct take-off point
b A ground line directly underneath the fence encourages a closer take-off

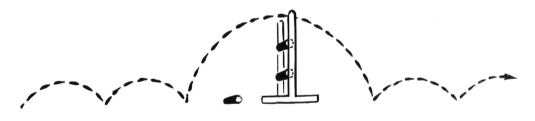

a

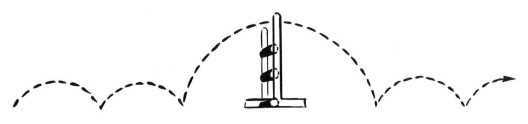

b

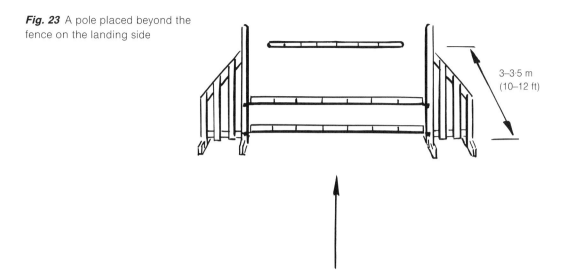

Fig. 23 A pole placed beyond the fence on the landing side

3–3·5 m
(10–12 ft)

keep the horse straight. The advantage of this exercise is that the horse does not know whether there are poles on the landing side, and, not wanting to take the risk of standing on them, the intelligent horse learns to jump and land straight **(fig. 24)**.

- A pole used as a ground line on the landing as well as the take-off side **(fig. 25)** helps the horse to:

(a) jump wider over the fence, producing a bigger arc

(b) make up more ground over the fence. Some horses do not jump far enough over the fence, which can leave insufficient room for the hindlegs to clear it. By opening the distance between the back rail of the fence and the ground line on the landing side, the horse can see that he must jump wider in order to clear the pole on the ground. To do this, he has to lengthen and lower his neck, which allows him to use his back and hindquarters to greater effect.

All these exercises are meant for training purposes only. They are designed to encourage the horse to make the best possible use of himself, and to correct any faults that he may have developed. Be sure to use the appropriate exercise for the fault, and above all, if you are in doubt, seek advice from a knowledgeable person. Remember that many jumping problems stem from an incorrect or unsuitable approach. It is your responsibility to ensure that the canter is rhythmical, energetic and balanced at all times. The line of approach must ensure that the horse is kept straight, balanced through

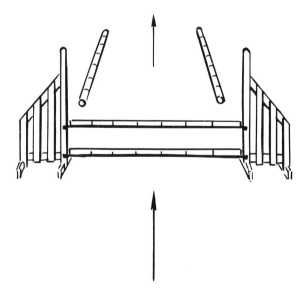

Fig. 24 Poles placed at 90° to the wings on the landing side

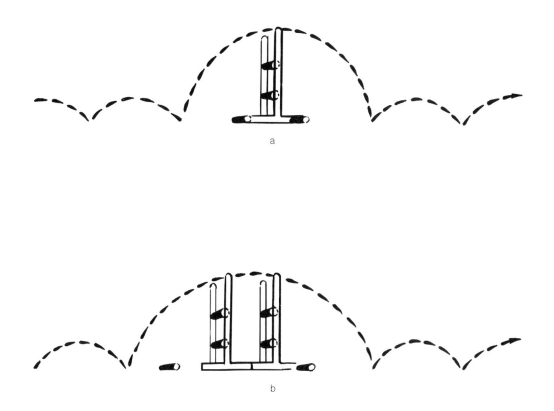

a

b

Fig. 25 A pole used as a ground line on the take-off
and landing side
a An upright fence
b A parallel fence

the turns, and in front of the leg or up to
the bridle; it is up to you to learn to feel the
rhythm and be able to shorten or lengthen
the stride where necessary.

With good early training and practice,
all these factors will start to become
second nature to you and your horse, so
that they become an integral part of your
approach to riding across country over
testing obstacles.

Training the horse to jump accurately

Once the horse has learned to canter in
straight lines and you are able to adjust
the canter so that the balance and impulsion can be altered, it is possible to ride a
horse to a specific point. Whatever type of
jumping you are doing, be it grid work,
show jumping or cross country, always
train your eye on the part of the fence that
you wish to jump. In this way, you will
learn to ride accurately on the approach
and through a combination or series of
fences.

When you are jumping poles painted in
bands of colour, it is easy to focus your eye
on a particular coloured section and ride
accurately to it, but for cross-country
jumping a different method is used. When
a fence is situated on a downhill slope, a
landmark on the horizon can be used to
guide you on to the correct line for the
approach. When you walk the course, pick
out an object that is clearly visible, and
not something that may be obscured by the
spectators on the day of the competition
(fig. 26). When it is necessary to ride

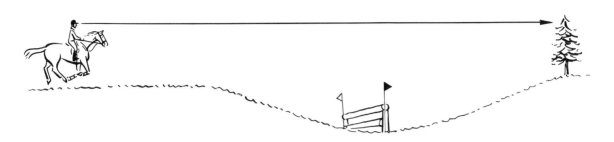

Fig. 26 An obvious landmark such as a tree can be used to guide you on the correct line for a fence

through a series of corners or turns, the posts used for stringing the course provide a good guide.

There are numerous ways of picking part of a fence on which to focus. If you intend to jump a post-and-rail fence in the middle, for example, focus on the central post or the string used for securing the rails. To jump a fence at any other given point, pick out something on the fence or beyond it that is easy to recognize from at least ten strides away. What you choose to focus on is immaterial, as long as you learn to ride accurately to a given point. If you cannot do this, jumping corners, combinations and arrowheads will be impossible. In other words, training yourself to ride accurately must begin at home.

How to build a corner

Small corners can be built using poles and drums. First of all, practise jumping an upright with one end supported by an oil drum instead of a jump stand. Jump the upright at 90° to the pole and as close to the drum as you can. If your horse runs past the jump, you have not kept him channelled between hand and leg, and your approach is not straight. If this is not the problem and the horse is being naughty, place an obstacle such as a large branch next to the drum to act as a wing to hold him in. Always be certain to ride a

TECHNIQUES TO PRACTISE

- Begin by jumping fences in the middle. It is helpful to have somebody on the ground to check that you have jumped the fence where you said you were going to! You may be unaware of how inaccurate you are.
- Practise cantering to fences either down the left- or right-hand side, trying to be specific and accurate.
- Canter to fences on an angle, from left to right and right to left, taking great care not to waver from your intended line of approach. If you are jumping fences with wings, try replacing the wings with oil drums to see how accurate you are without them.
- Practise jumping a variety of narrow (approximately 1 metre [3 ft] wide). Some horses do not understand how to jump these at first, but with a well-balanced, slow, energetic canter and a positive attitude on your part, success will soon come.
- Build three or four fences with true distances between them, but set them off at an angle from each other so that a definite line has to be ridden unless run-outs are to be encountered (fig. 27).
- Build small corners with poles and oil drums, and, when accuracy and a bold approach are guaranteed, open up the angle bit by bit (see below).

line which shows the horse the fence, and not the way out to the side.

Once the upright has been mastered, introduce a second rail behind the first **(fig. 28)**. Place one end on the drum, and support the other end with a jump stand

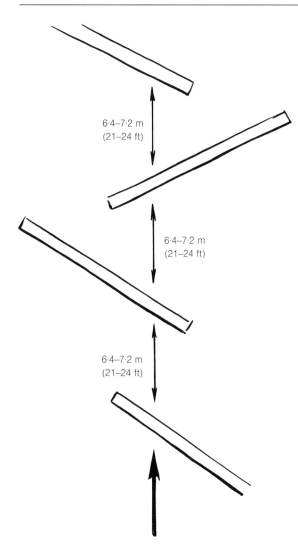

6·4–7·2 m
(21–24 ft)

6·4–7·2 m
(21–24 ft)

6·4–7·2 m
(21–24 ft)

and cup in the usual way. This back rail should be a little higher than the front rail so that the horse can see it. Keeping the approach at 90° to the front rail, make the angle for the corner by opening up the back rail a little at a time.

When both you and the horse have become confident and accurate in your approach and jump, the front rail can be moved to open up the angle of the corner. This changes the appearance of the fence, as the front rail will no longer be jumped at a 90° angle if the same line of approach as before is used. Instead, the corner is now jumped at 90° to the bisected angle **(fig. 29)**. When a corner is very wide it is not possible to approach the front rail at 90° as you will land in the middle of the two rails, which will do nothing for the horse's confidence, not to mention your own!

When a corner fence is encountered on a cross-country course, you must try to find a line of approach where:

- the ground does not slope away and carry you past the fence
- the angle is not too wide
- the approach shows the horse the fence and not the daylight to the side of it, which will encourage a run-out
- the approach or the ground does not carry the horse too far down the fence,

Fig. 27 (*Left*) A row of fences with true distances between them, but set off at different angles

Fig. 28 (*Right*) A second rail can be added behind the first to create an extra challenge

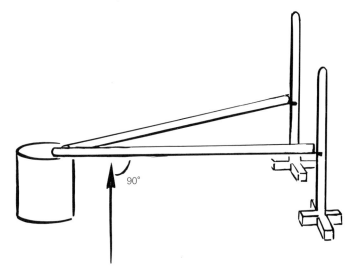

90°

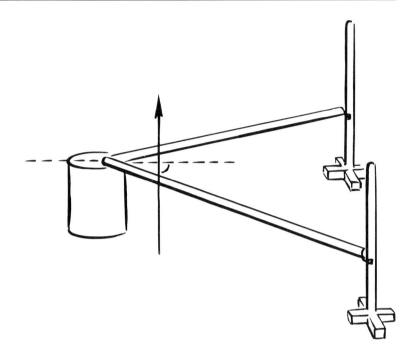

Fig. 29 When the horse is confident and accurate in his approach, the front rail can be moved to open up the angle. A right-handed corner can be built in the same way

which could result in the horse landing in the middle of the corner
• There is enough light and room for the horse to land. If there is a big tree or a wall three or four strides after your intended landing spot, for instance, your horse will probably shy off the line as he thinks he is in danger of running into the offending object, so a clearer, more obvious line is necessary

Jumping into wooded areas

For a horse to jump successfully into wooded areas, he must be familiar with changes of light. Horses often find jumping from light to dark quite alarming, and when out hacking, wooded areas are always full of hobgoblins. It is therefore a good idea, if possible, to familiarize your horse with the different smells and sounds before he encounters the situation when competing, or he may spend so much time spooking that it will be difficult to get his attention. Try to trot and canter into and out of woods so that he becomes confident before he is asked to jump into a wood.

It is important to keep the horse well-balanced and the canter energetic so that, when he is asked to jump into a wood, it will be possible to create more energy if he starts to back off. An approach in a flat-out gallop is unsuitable as, if the horse backs off, he will soon become unbalanced because he was going too fast originally. In this situation, he will either stop, fall over the fence or run straight past it in an uncontrollable way. If he does manage to jump the fence, the track through the wood may well be twisty and, as he will still be going too fast to negotiate the turns, he may lose his footing and fall over. It is rather like driving a car into a series of bends at too great a speed, and losing control by the second or third bend. When riding across country, therefore, and particularly into a wooded area, always go at a speed that is suitable for the oncoming situation.

SUMMARY

- Loose schooling is an ideal way of introducing the young horse to jumping, as he can concentrate entirely on what he is doing without the encumbrance of your weight.
- Poles on the ground make a good preliminary to jumping when ridden. The horse must never be allowed to rush the poles, but should learn to approach them quietly and calmly.
- The horse's balance on landing over a fence is as important as when he is taking off, and should be taught at an early stage. On landing, ride away in a straight line, preferably in canter, so that the horse learns to go forward and to regain his balance as quickly as possible. This is an important lesson for future cross-country riding, when combination fences will test the horse's ability to string together a series of fences.
- Always keep the jump training interesting by introducing different types of fences, but be careful never to over-face the horse.
- The quality of the canter is the basis of all successful jumping. A good canter is often a matter of creating a little more impulsion and of keeping the horse together by controlling and condensing the stride. This is particularly important on a course when combinations are sited on undulating terrain.
- Always train your eye on the part of the fence that you wish to jump. This will produce the accurate approach and take-off needed to negotiate a combination or demanding fence.
- The inexperienced horse should never be asked to negotiate fences that are designed to trick him, as he may lose confidence. At the same time, it is vital to teach the horse to jump accurately over his fences from an early stage, so that he will be able to cope with fences such as corners, arrowheads and combinations on a course.
- If you encounter a fence more advanced than your horse's stage of training, jump the easier alternative. At this stage, risks and heroics are not called for, especially if one day you wish to succeed at the highest level.

3
THE RIDER

People of all shapes and sizes ride across country. Although we are not all ideal shapes, it is possible to develop a way of riding which enables us to ride safely and successfully, and helps to bring out the best in our horses at the same time. The most important single factor for all riders is to be able to remain in balance, not only in the basic paces on level ground but also while negotiating fences at differing speeds, when riding up and down hills, and probably most difficult of all, when things go wrong (11) and (12). If, as well as training and developing the horse correctly, you learn to ride with a balanced seat, you will always be able to help the horse and hopefully never hinder him. Achieving this goal takes time, but, unless you master this balanced seat, success both in training and the competition world will always elude you.

It is also important to be as fit as possible. Cross-country riding is very demanding, and there is nothing worse than seeing a rider flopping about on a horse, especially towards the end of a round. This is the time when the horse needs the most help, and an unfit rider will only be a hindrance to an already tiring horse. If this situation sounds all too familiar to you, then it is in your own interests to become fit. Your poor physical state may be attributable to many factors –

diet, lack of exercise, a shortage of time – but whatever the reason, you must try to rectify the problem or your horse's confidence will suffer. Eating sensibly and taking regular exercise are the only ways of attaining a level of fitness comparable to that of your horse.

Establishing the basic riding position

Working on the lunge is probably the most effective way in which to start developing your seat. As the horse is controlled by the person doing the lungeing, you have the opportunity to concentrate entirely on your position. If the lungeing is to be successful, however, the horse, trainer, exercises and their frequency all need to be taken into account.

11 This young horse has misjudged the fence in the water. The rider is hopelessly in front of the movement and her lower legs have slipped

12 The rider has realized her mistake and has quickly sat up and regained a secure lower-leg position. Although she made a mistake initially, she has allowed the horse the freedom of his head and neck throughout

POINTS TO REMEMBER

- The horse should be well-established in his way of working on the lunge.
- He must stay out on the end of the lunge line so that the circle is true and does not become too small, or you will become dizzy and find it difficult to keep your balance.
- His walk, trot and canter should be balanced and rhythmical.
- His trot should not be too springy or you will be thrown out of the saddle too much.
- He should be a suitable size and width for you.
- The saddle should fit you.
- The horse should be responsive to commands used by the trainer as a means of control.
- The trainer should be experienced in handling the lunge equipment and controlling the horse.
- The trainer must be clear with his or her instructions.
- Work must be carried out equally on both reins.
- The exercises must be geared towards improving your riding position, but must never be beyond your capabilities.
- Daily lungeing is a good idea if your position is very insecure and if time permits; otherwise a weekly lunge will be beneficial, even for the well-established rider.

The choice of exercises should be related to specific problems. Work on one at a time, slowly and quietly, as the root problem is often tension and lack of suppleness. It is important to ensure that each exercise does not create tension and tightening in another part of the body.

The horse should be warmed up in side reins for five to ten minutes before you begin. Undo the side reins, get on, and then do them up again. Work first with stirrups and reins in walk and trot in both directions so that the trainer can assess your basic position and identify any obvious problems. The following exercises cover most problems and are of benefit to all riders.

Exercises for the upper body

Knot the reins and secure them under a neck strap (the novice rider can hold on to the pommel of the saddle with the outside hand while the inside arm exercises). Carry out each exercise in walk on both reins. Rest for a minute after each exercise by letting your arms hang down by your sides.

1. Hunch your shoulders up towards your ears, and then slowly rotate them backward in a circular motion (**fig. 30**).
2. Place your fingers on top of your shoulders and rotate the arms backward, taking your elbows as far back as possible and keeping your upper body straight without twisting at the waist.
3. Slowly circle the inside arm backwards in big circles.
4. Fold both arms in front of your chest, and then push your elbows backwards while keeping your arms parallel to the ground. Extend your arms out to the side, so that your shoulders are back and your chest is out (**fig. 31**).
5. Take both arms out in front of you so that your fingers are at eye level, and parallel to the ground (**fig. 32**). Slowly rotate your upper body to the inside, and then back to the middle. Make sure that you keep your hips level, so that you only turn from the waist. The trainer should also check that your fingers remain level, that your lower leg is not swinging and that you have not collapsed to one side. Take your arms above your head so that your fingers are level, then rotate your upper body from the waist to the inside of the circle. Again, the trainer must ensure

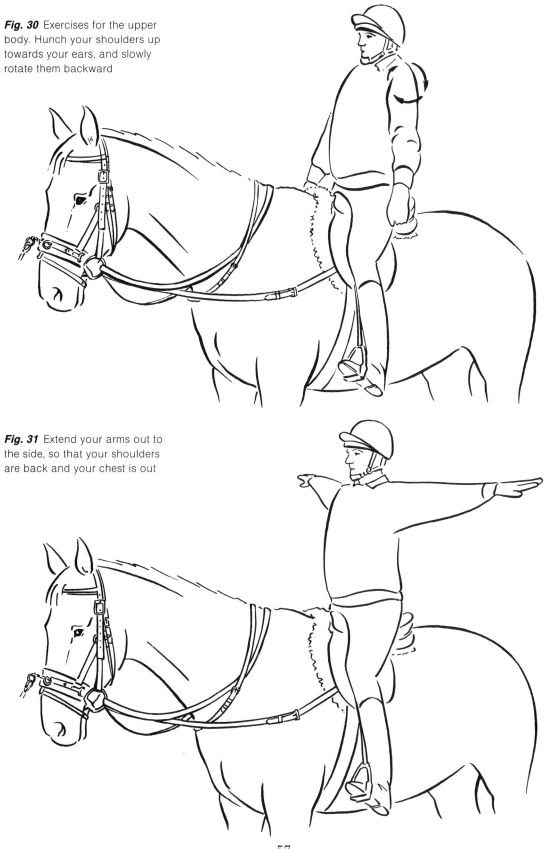

Fig. 30 Exercises for the upper body. Hunch your shoulders up towards your ears, and slowly rotate them backward

Fig. 31 Extend your arms out to the side, so that your shoulders are back and your chest is out

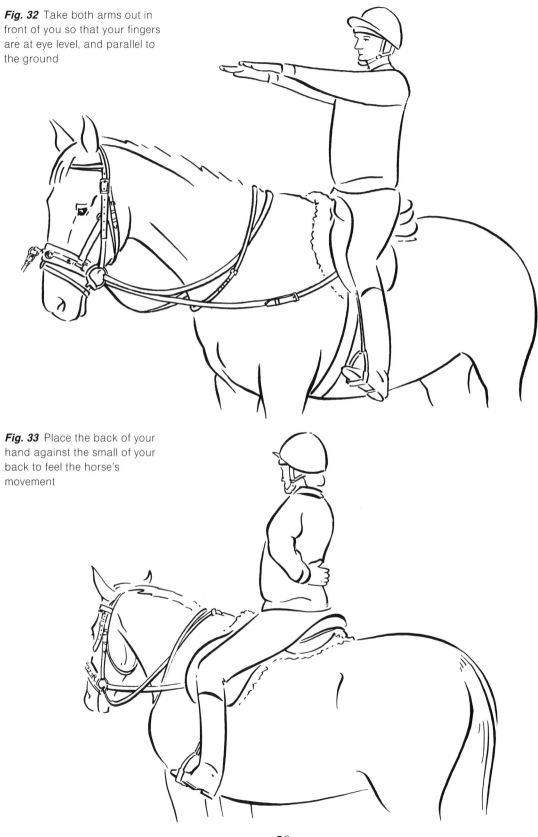

Fig. 32 Take both arms out in front of you so that your fingers are at eye level, and parallel to the ground

Fig. 33 Place the back of your hand against the small of your back to feel the horse's movement

that you are not collapsing at the hips or dropping a shoulder.

6. Hold your arms out to the side of your upper body, parallel to the ground. With one arm at a time, lean over and touch your toes on the opposite side, then lean forward from the waist and touch your horse's poll, making sure that your legs do not swing backward. It is best to do this exercise in halt initially.

7. Place the back of your hand against the small of your back so that you can feel the horse's movement. Your back should remain supple so that the horse's natural movement is not restricted (**fig. 33**). This is a good way to feel whether the upper body has become tight in either walk, trot or canter.

Your upper body should remain free from tension at all times. Your head, with your chin tucked in and not jutting out, should be directly above your shoulders, and your eyes should focus in the direction in which you wish to go. Your shoulders should be level with the horse's shoulders. On a circle or through a turn, your inside shoulder should be back to lead the horse's inside shoulder around the turn. Carry your shoulders tall, with your chest out, and directly above your hips; rounded shoulders lead to a collapsed upper body which encourages the horse to go on the forehand and lean on the bit.

Your upper arms should be bent enough to allow your lower arms to be in a direct line with the reins from your hands to the horse's mouth, and your elbows should hang loosely against your sides. Keep your hands level and approximately 10–15 cm (3–4 ins) apart, with closed fingers and wrists relaxed and slightly rounded with the thumbs on top.

Your stomach should feel as though it is pushing into your spine: this will keep your lower back soft and free to move with the swing of the horse's steps. Your pelvis should be forward, or your back will hollow and stiffen your upper body.

The above exercises can also be carried out each day without the lunge.

Exercises for the lower body

Cross the stirrups in front of the saddle (the novice rider can still hold on to the pommel with the outside hand). Practise the following exercises in walk initially, and then in trot and in canter if the horse is well-balanced and when you are more confident. Keep the circle large, or you will become dizzy and the horse will lose his balance. Try to sit in the middle of the saddle and equally on both seat bones.

1. Hold on to the pommel with both hands. Shrug both legs to let them hang loose and relaxed, and then rotate your feet and ankles slowly in circles in both directions.

2. Take each leg backward so that your lower leg is towards the horse's quarters, and swing it forward from the hip, keeping your leg as long as possible and your upper body still.

3. Bend your inside leg so that the heel comes into the back of your thigh, and grasp your ankle with the corresponding hand (**fig. 34**). Bring your heel as close to your thigh as possible, and think of pushing your knee to the ground. Be careful that your upper body does not tip forward or fall to one side. This exercise can only be carried out in halt and walk.

4. Hold on to the pommel with both hands, and lift each leg away from the saddle at the hip (**fig. 35**). Do this with one leg at a time and then both together, hold for a short time, then rest and repeat. Your seat bones should remain in contact with the saddle, and your upper body should not fall backwards. Let your

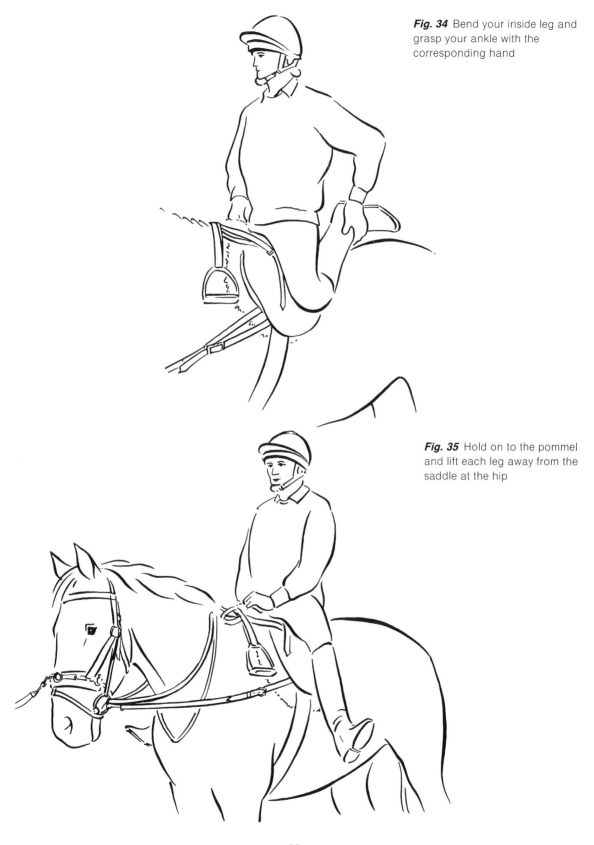

Fig. 34 Bend your inside leg and grasp your ankle with the corresponding hand

Fig. 35 Hold on to the pommel and lift each leg away from the saddle at the hip

Fig. 36 The correct lower-leg position, with the weight in the heels

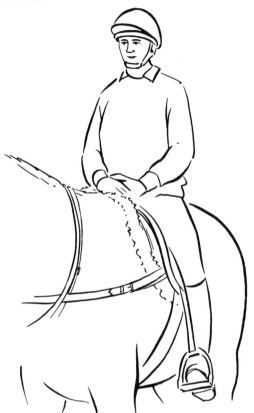

legs go long and loose to finish. This exercise can be carried out in walk, trot and canter.

5. To place your lower legs in the correct riding position, keep your hips level and let your legs stretch down as far as possible. Then, by relaxing your hips and thighs, bend your knees so that the insides of your calf muscles come into contact with the horse's sides. Your ankles should be flexed so that your toes are higher than your heels and pointing slightly outward **(fig. 36)**.

Your thighs and knees should be as loose as possible, or your lower legs will not stay in contact with the horse's sides in trot and canter. As soon as the thighs and knees become tense and tight, your lower legs and heels will draw up and away from the horse's sides, and it will be difficult to feel your seat bones and to keep your upper body relaxed. If you try to keep your lower legs too long, they will draw up when you use them, so always try to keep them at a length from which they can be used without the heels or knees drawing up.

Eventually it should become possible for you to walk, trot and canter on the lunge without holding on to the pommel or being reliant on the stirrups. It is all to do with staying in balance and being relaxed. Human nature dictates that, when we are riding, as soon as something goes wrong or confidence is lost, we become tense. This makes it difficult to remain in balance, as we are gripping upward with our lower legs and usually tipping forward, therefore defying the laws of gravity. If the body stiffens up anywhere the balance will be affected, so, even when you are hacking, go through some of the exercises.

If your upper body is allowed to become stiff, it can be the root of the problems connected with developing a secure lower-leg position, so be sure to keep both the upper and lower body relaxed and free from tension by practising the exercises. Practise little by little, and you will eventually find your balance. When being lunged, hold on to the pommel to start with, and let go with the inside hand and then the outside hand when you feel that your balance is good enough. If you feel your body tighten and your legs drawing up, let your legs hang loosely and take your thighs away from the saddle so that you can feel your seat bones again. From there, re-establish your lower-leg position and check that your upper body has not stiffened as well.

Your lower body should also remain relaxed and free from tension at all times. Your hips should be level, as any collapsing will encourage the horse to carry

himself in a crooked way. Your hip jonts should be kept loose, or your thighs will be tight around the horse's ribs; from a horse's point of view, this must create the same feeling as a human giving someone a piggy back whose thighs grip round their waist like a vice. This feeling can only make the horse hollow away from the unpleasant grip. Any muscle on your thighs should be pushed to the back so that it lies behind the thighs, and not next to the horse.

Your knees should be relaxed, and kept open and away from the horse's sides; this will help you to keep the correct lower-leg position with the weight down in your heels. Flexing your ankles, with your toes facing a little to the outside, will allow you to maintain this position. Your heels should be in a direct line with your shoulders and hips, and your toes in a line with your knees.

Moving the horse away from the lower leg will help to establish a secure and effective position. Start in walk, and increase and decrease the size of the circle by squeezing with the appropriate lower leg. Build up the exercise in trot and canter, making sure all the time that you do not tighten or draw up your leg.

As an end result, it should be possible to maintain the correct position once you have taken back your stirrups and reins (13). In walk you should be able to sit and stand up in your stirrups without your shoulders tipping forward, or your thighs and knees tightening and your lower legs coming away from the horse's sides. If you can keep your balance, try the same exercise in trot and then in canter. If you can do this exercise, you have acquired a secure lower-leg position. Take back your reins and see whether it is possible to keep

13 The correct riding position. The rider is sitting up straight and relaxed, with an excellent lower-leg position and the weight in her heels

your hands in the correct riding position in walk, rising and sitting trot and canter without them swinging about. If you can do this, you are well on the way to establishing an independent seat and being able to ride successfully across country.

Establishing the cross-country position

When riding across country, the angles between the hips, knees and ankles are closed up by shortening the stirrups. This will push your bottom towards the back of the saddle while your knees come more forward, so it is important to have a saddle with adequately forward-cut flaps and a large enough seat.

When the stirrups are shortened, it must be possible for you to remain in balance, especially when you lighten your seat and bring your bottom out of the saddle. The upper body inclines forward from the waist, and, to prevent you from falling on to the horse's neck, your lower legs must remain secure with the weight in the heels (14). One of the most important aspects of jumping is being able to allow the horse the freedom to use his head and neck as much or as little as he wishes during the airborne phase of the jump, and this can only be achieved with good balance and the correct riding position.

In a standing position, a person's centre of mass is behind the stomach and in front of the spine, and is evenly balanced mainly by the pull of gravity and because our legs and feet are positioned directly underneath our upper body. This stance can be related to the dressage position, where the upper body still remains vertical. To adapt to the cross-country position, the upper body is inclined forward from the waist when the horse is galloping, and during the airborne phase of the jump the rider's

15 With the weight in the heels, the upper body can be moved to any position and remain in balance

16 The same exercise is repeated with the weight on the toes instead of the heels. When the upper body is brought forward, it is impossible to remain in balance

arm is pushed towards the horse's mouth. This means that the centre of mass is further forward than when standing or riding in a dressage position, and, unless the upper is counterbalanced by the lower body, a loss of balance will occur and the upper body will topple forward.

Imagine sitting in a chair with an upright back. If you have your weight in your heels, you can move your upper body where you wish, bending forward from the waist or moving from side to side without ever losing your balance **(15)**. Relate this to jumping: on take-off you can extend

14 (*Left*) A secure lower-leg position means that the rider can remain in balance when she lightens her seat, so that the hands become independent

your arms forward towards the horse's mouth so that he has as much freedom of his head and neck as he wishes, while you remain in balance because the lower legs are still in position and counterbalancing the upper body, which is further forward than before.

Now imagine the upright chair again, and repeat the same exercise by standing on your toes instead of your heels. If you bring your upper body forward it will be impossible to remain in balance, and you will fall forward until you put a hand out to save yourself **(16)**. Relate this to jumping: on take-off you can extend your arms forward, but your lower legs will shoot backward, and therefore cannot help to keep you in balance **(17)**. To regain

17 If the lower legs shoot backward while jumping, they become completely ineffective and balance will be lost

balance, you would have to rest your hands on the horse's neck, making it impossible for him to use his head and neck as you have caused a restriction. Now he will be in trouble, as, not only have you prevented him from using his head and neck (which means that he cannot use his forehand correctly on take-off), but you are also preventing him from using his back and hindquarters during the airborne phase of the jump. As a result, he may not be able to make sufficient height or width over the fence, or be able to get his legs on the ground for the landing phase, causing a possible fall.

It is clear from these examples that the only way in which a horse can jump to the best of his ability is if you do not hinder him, so it is of ultimate importance to learn to ride with a secure, balanced, independent seat so that you are able to remain in balance with the horse on the approach, in the air, on landing and in the getaway. The length of stirrup is a personal choice, but the stirrup leathers should hang vertically, and your lower legs should remain in contact with the horse's sides at all times, with low heels and flexible ankles.

A good exercise to help in establishing the balance is to shorten your stirrups to your usual cross-country length. Lighten your seat, bring your upper body forward a little from the waist, and see whether you can remain in balance while keeping your hands away from the horse's neck (18). If you cannot keep the balance, check that your stirrups are not too long or too short. Most people ride across country with stirrups that are too long, making a secure lower-leg position impossible.

Start in walk and progress through the paces. Whenever you have to rest your

hands on the horse's neck, you will know that you have lost your balance. Keep your knees soft and open, as this will help to keep the ankles flexed and the heels low. Once you have achieved balance within the basic paces, practise the exercise on undulating ground, and while increasing and decreasing the speed in canter.

When cantering downhill, keep your shoulders up and back to help you with the balance. Your lower legs can be allowed a little more forward to help to prevent the horse from leaning on the forehand and running into the ground. When cantering uphill, make sure that your lower legs do not slip backward with your upper body tipping too far forward, or the horse will drop behind the leg or the bridle and the impulsion will fade.

Your position on the way to a fence

When galloping across country, you should have your weight out of the saddle and off the horse's back, so that he covers the ground with the minimum of effort. Your lower legs should remain still, and in a position which allows the stirrup leathers to hang vertically. Your upper body should be inclined slightly forward, but not so low as to be almost horizontal. Your shoulders, head and neck should be kept up, and your hands close to the horse's neck and just in front of the withers. When cantering or galloping, you should be able to feel the rhythm of the strides coming up underneath the horse, and with every stride you should feel your own weight dropping into your lower legs and heels. Your arms should be slightly flexible to allow the horse to move his head and neck within the rhythm of the strides.

It is important at all times to be aware of the terrain and the condition of the going, so that you can make minor adjustments through your body to the horse's speed. These adjustments must always be within

18 This rider is in the correct position, and is therefore able to raise herself out of the saddle and remain in balance with light hands

the rhythm of the stride, so that the horse remains in good balance. When approaching a fence, you need to decide beforehand what sort of pace you want. If you are approaching a combination with short distances between the fences, for example, you will require a slower speed, with the horse taking shorter strides than when galloping. If you are approaching a combination with longer distances, you will need a longer stride.

Whatever the type of fence, the pace must be balanced, rhythmical and energetic with the horse between your legs and hands. This is especially important if there

is a combination or series of fences on an angle or a continuous curve, or where the fences are narrow. Even if you are approaching a straightforward fence such as an ascending spread (see page 88), where accuracy is less crucial, it is still important to set the horse up so that he has good rhythm and balance, even though the strides are still quite long and the speed quite fast. A horse galloping flat out and unbalanced on the approach to a fence, with an unbalanced rider, is very unlikely to recover if he makes a mistake; but if a balanced horse and rider make a mistake, they usually manage to remain on their feet on the landing side.

It should by now be clear that the approach to cross-country fences is a matter of maintaining a rhythmical, energetic, balanced pace. Whether this is

19 By sitting up and keeping the shoulders up, the rider's weight is off the horse's back, producing a good, even stride

a collected canter or a controlled gallop will depend on the type of fence, the condition of the going, the terrain, the horse's experience and what is to follow. The main point to remember is to sit up and keep your shoulders up. Whether you sit lightly on or above the saddle is of little importance, as long as you are not sitting against the horse, as this will encourage him to hollow away from your weight and may break the rhythm of his stride **(19)**. Keep your lower legs in contact with the horse's side: passively if he has enough energy within the pace, but actively if he starts to back off a fence and lose impul-

sion or confidence. Keep your hands low and quiet, and in a position in which they do not restrict the horse's natural movement. If he wavers on the approach, the hand on the corresponding side can be opened away from the neck to encourage him to stay in a straight line. As you gain experience you will learn to feel when there is any alteration which, if not corrected, will affect the quality of the jump.

Ultimately, it is experience that will teach you the approach required for every type of fence you meet on a course, but correct training and the ability to adjust your pace and position on the approach will give you the best possible chance of negotiating the fences cleanly. In this way, you will soon develop the confidence to know how you want the horse to feel on the approach to each individual fence.

Fig. 37 The sequence over a fence

       The approach
b–c   The take-off
d   The airborne phase
e   The landing
f   The getaway

More detailed information on riding different types of fences can be found in Chapter 5.

The sequence over a fence

The take-off occurs when the horse first lifts his forehand from the ground, closely followed by his hindquarters **(fig. 37)**. It is important not to throw your upper body forward on the approach, or before the horse has left the ground. If you do so, you may unbalance the horse, interfere with his concentration, and make it difficult for him to raise his forehand as your weight suddenly drops forward.

If you throw your weight forward in anticipation of the take-off, the horse will often not take off at the same time, leaving you hopelessly in front of the movement. In addition, if he has second thoughts about the fence, you cannot drive him forward as you will already be halfway up his neck and in no position to help him. Think of the withers coming up to meet you on take-off, not the other way round, and of allowing your hands forward towards the horse's mouth so that the amount of release is determined by how much he wishes to use his neck. In this way your upper body has to come forward, because your arms have moved forward and your upper body has to follow through. If you simply think of folding forward from the waist, your hands may still remain just in front of the withers, preventing the horse from using his head and neck at leisure.

Keep your shoulders parallel to the ground and your head and neck to the front, and look straight ahead. If you lean to one side you are likely to unbalance the horse and he may jump crookedly, and if you look on the ground instead of forward you are likely to end up there! Your lower legs should remain in position and not fly backward on take-off, or you will become unbalanced. Try not to over-react with your upper body over the fence, as too much movement here can unbalance the horse and may also encourage him to be too quick through the air. In addition, the more you move your upper body during the take-off and airborne phases, the more you must move it back to regain your original position by the getaway stage.

During the landing phase, keep your lower legs forward and your seat back but light to help to balance the horse. If you adopt this 'safety' position, you will not be thrown over the horse's head if he pecks or stumbles. Keep your shoulders up, your back soft and your hands low to help to absorb the impact of the landing. This position will also help you to pick up the horse if he is in danger of losing his balance and falling over his forelegs.

SUMMARY

- Your own fitness is important, as well as that of the horse. At the end of a round, an unfit rider will only be a hindrance to a tiring horse.
- Regular work on the lunge will benefit even the well-established rider, and is particularly helpful for improving an insecure seat.
- The most important aspect of cross-country riding is being able to remain in balance with a secure seat while negotiating fences at different speeds, when riding up and down hills and – most importantly – when things go wrong. A horse galloping too fast wth an unbalanced rider is very unlikely to recover if he makes a mistake, but a balanced horse and rider usually manage to remain on their feet on the landing side.
- Between fences, your weight should be kept out of saddle and off the horse's back, so that he covers the ground with the minimum of effort.
- It is you who has walked the course, so it is your job to think ahead and to present the horse correctly at every type of fence so that he has the best possible chance of jumping it.
- Cross-country jumping is all about trying to make the right adjustments, and, from there, moving your body as little as possible. It is really common sense that the less movement you make, the easier it is for the horse to carry you.

Part 2
CROSS-COUNTRY RIDING

4

CROSS-COUNTRY SCHOOLING

Once your horse has been introduced to different natural hazards at home, such as ditches, logs and water, and is jumping a variety of fences confidently in canter, he is ready to encounter his first cross-country school.

Choose a venue at which there is a variety of small, well-built, inviting fences. (A list of venues in Britain and the USA can be found on pages 166 to 171). It is a good idea to take an experienced horse with you, to give you a lead if necessary. Allow sufficient time to warm up your horse properly. A new environment may make him a little tense and excited, but, if he is allowed a few minutes to adjust to his new setting, and is warmed up in the same way as he is at home, he should be able to relate to this and gain confidence from it. Unless he feels confident, you will soon come unstuck over the fences. Establish a forward-going, balanced and rhythmic canter before you begin jumping, and be sure that the horse is listening to you.

Starting to jump

Begin by jumping one or two straight-forward fences, such as a log, an ascending spread and a row of tyres (20). Check the quality of the canter, and always remem-ber to re-establish the canter after each jump. If the horse appears a little green, do not progress to anything more complic-ated until he feels confident over the easy fences. If he seems to be coping well, do not be worried by a little over-enthusiasm at this stage, as there will be a fence some-where on the course that will make him think!

Once you have jumped the easy fences, try putting three or four together, but keep the complexity of the fences and the terrain simple. Try to maintain the well-balanced, forward-thinking canter between the fences. Young horses tend to wobble from fence to fence at first, but, once they learn to move on from one fence to the next, a balanced canter becomes easier to sustain. On the approach, con-centrate on riding to the middle of each fence, using your legs to channel the horse forward and keeping your hands steady with an even contact on his mouth. If you maintain a definite idea of how you wish the horse to approach and jump each fence, the feeling will transmit itself to the horse and he will soon improve his way of going.

Having jumped a few fences, praise the horse and let him have a walk around. The stress of a journey and new surroundings will use up his energy quickly, so give him plenty of breaks to prevent him from

20 Every schooling session should begin with an easy fence such as this row of tyres. This horse is wearing an American gag with a nylon mouthpiece because he is very strong and difficult to keep in an outline

becoming tired and making a mistake. After walking for five minutes or so, establish the canter again and jump a few more fences. Start with a straightforward one to get the horse going, and then jump three or four different types of fences – ideally, there will be a good variety from which to choose, which will not over-face the horse.

Combinations, banks, ditches and water

At this stage, straightforward combinations, banks, ditches and water may be introduced. With combinations, make sure that the distances are suitable before jumping them – for instance, banks must not be too steep or too narrow to jump on and off **(21–5)**. A small ditch on the take-off side of a hedge is ideal for the young horse, as is a small trakhener (see page 96), but the pole or log must be low and the ditch must not be wide. At a water fence, first have a paddle. After this, trot in and out a

21 (*Left*) This bank is of suitable dimensions for an inexperienced horse. Both horse and rider are jumping on to it with confidence, although the reins are a little long and the rider's lower legs have slipped back behind the girth

22 (*Below*) A young horse jumping off a small bank. The horse has lengthened his head and neck and the rider has allowed him plenty of rein, although moving her arms forward towards the mouth would have helped her to keep the reins a little shorter

23 (*Top right*) This young horse has jumped higher over the bank and is a little unbalanced – note the hindlegs. The rider has allowed the horse the freedom of the head and neck, but is a little behind the movement – probably as a precaution in case the horse pecks on landing

24 (*Bottom right*) The horse has landed a little steeply and out of balance – note how far back the forelegs are. The rider has braced her back a little too much, but her lower legs are in a secure position and she has not interfered with the horse's outline

few times, and then jump a little log or step down into the water **(26)**.

Coffins

If there is a small coffin, explain it to the horse step by step and he will soon understand. At home he will probably have encountered a ditch on its own, so jump the ditch of the coffin first. Approach diagonally across the ditch so that the horse can see where he is being asked to jump **(27)**. Do not face him at the rail, as he may be confused at this stage and may not be able to cope with jumping the ditch and then the rail. Once he has jumped the ditch with confidence, jump it straight so that he continues over the rail after the ditch. His jump training at home will give him confidence, as he will be able to relate to

25 The horse has regained her balance and self-carriage, but, as the rider has no contact, it would be very difficult to jump another fence in the next two strides. Until the bank can be negotiated more smoothly, it would not be sensible to introduce another element

jumps with one or two strides between them.

Once the horse has mastered the two parts, the first rail can be introduced. Be sure to keep him straight, balanced and with enough impulsion. If you run out of impulsion at the first element, the horse will struggle to jump the rail, the ditch and the exit rail, or he may stop altogether, which will be bad for his confidence. It is up to you to give the horse the best chance of jumping the fences by ensuring that the approach is well-prepared. If you have

26 Once the horse is confident in water, a small log can be jumped. The rider's lower legs are secure, and she has allowed the horse the freedom of her head and neck. The young horse's forelegs are not a pair – a sign of greenness

done your early training correctly at home, a coffin should not present a problem at this stage, unless the terrain, distances or ditch are an unsuitable introduction to this type of fence.

Steps

Having already jumped a bank, steps are a natural progression. Make sure that they are not too steep and that the distance between them is generous. When jumping down steps, maintain your balance by keeping your lower legs forward and your shoulders up. This is especially important with young horses, as they are often confused by steps at first and need a

27 The individual elements of a coffin should be introduced to the horse before he is asked to jump them together, to avoid confusion

minute or two to work them out. They often jump one and then stop dead, so if you are leaning forward you will probably end up round your horse's neck and in no position to encourage him forward. At this stage, approach downhill steps in a forward-thinking trot. An approach in canter can be too quick, as the horse may jump too far off the first step, landing out of balance and therefore in no position from which to jump the rest of the steps.

As long as the steps are not steep, going up is not too difficult as long as you keep the horse balanced and straight. Keep your legs on the girth, with your upper body slightly forward and your seat a little further back so that you do not get left behind and become a burden to the horse. An approach in canter is ideal for uphill steps, as long as the impulsion is maintained. When jumping either up or down, it is important to land in balance after each step so that the horse is able to complete them. See page 111 for further advice on negotiating steps.

Horses are always taking us by surprise, so if your horse is greener than expected, jump a variety of straightforward fences in trot and with a lead if necessary. He will benefit greatly from this outing, and he can always come again and jump some of the more complex fences. On these occasions, as with the early training sessions, it is always better to do a small amount and to take your horse home feeling confident than to overdo it and to take home a nervous horse whose confidence has been eroded. With any level of horse, it is always worth remembering to start and finish your schooling session by jumping straightforward fences, so that you take home a confident horse.

In the early stages of your horse's career, he will benefit from cross-country schooling sessions or a hunter trial every

POINTS TO REMEMBER AT A COMPETITION

- Aim for a course that is smaller and easier than the horse is able to manage.
- The hustle and bustle of the competition may make him feel a little unsure of his surroundings.
- Try to time your arrival so that your horse does not have to stand in the lorry for hours, as the loudspeakers and competition atmosphere may unsettle him.
- Give yourself plenty of time to accustom the horse to the surroundings before you start working him in.
- The practice fence may become very poached, but the ground may be as bad on the course, so the horse must be familiar with it before he sets off.
- The aim of the outing is to give your horse a confidence-boosting round, in which he feels positive at each fence and maintains a good rhythm throughout.
- Remember to be generous with your praise.

two weeks if possible. This will not only improve his knowledge while he gains experience, but will also increase his fitness.

Once you have finished your round, wash the horse down and check for any cuts or minor injuries. Pick out his feet and remove the studs before leading him in hand for at least fifteen minutes to cool him off. Offer water at regular intervals after he has stopped blowing and continue until it is time to go home. When he is fully recovered, dry and warm, brush him to remove any traces of sweat, mud and dirt before you put him into the lorry. Give him a haynet to keep him quiet and relaxed.

The next day, trot him up to check for any unsoundness and, if all is well, turn him out for a few hours so that he can relax. If there is a problem, find out the cause and treat it accordingly. Always seek expert advice if the cause of the problem is uncertain.

Jumping after cross-country schooling or a competition

The next time you jump your horse, which should be at least four days after the competition or schooling day, it is a good idea to re-establish his basic work by jumping him in a schooling arca. This is because, after cross-country schooling or competitions, it is important to check that the horse's way of going is still correct for his stage of training. The canter strides may have become longer and flatter, and it may not be so easy to manoeuvre the canter in terms of increasing and decreasing the stride length while encouraging more engagement of the hindquarters.

It is therefore important at this stage still to spend considerable time on the horse's flat work, because, without a secure base from which to build, future progress will be limited. Work on the transitions (referring back to the early training exercises in Chapter 1), the acceptance of the bit and the way in which the horse works through from the leg to the hand. Be aware of any crookedness, stiffness or tension. Most horses love going across country as it gives them a sense of freedom, but it can be detrimental to their basic way of going on the flat, and to the correct technique over the fences learned in the early jump-training sessions, as outlined in Chapter 2. As the horse travels at a faster speed across country than he does when jumping in a school, his whole outline and stride are lengthened. As a result, his jumping technique may become longer and flatter, and, unless he is re-established in his way of going and good technique, he will never progress to jumping more advanced fences requiring accuracy, athleticism and the corrrect approach. Use the basic jumping exercises described in Chapter 2 to re-establish his technique.

If the canter strides have become longer and faster after going across country, the horse may make up too much distance between his fences. Never pull him off a fence or try to compress him by pulling on his mouth. Use the canter-trot transitions to improve the canter, but, if he still tries to make up too much ground when jumping, simply sit still without your upper body being pulled forward. If the horse then gets too close to the fences and knocks them down, he will soon learn to back off the fences and to shorten his outline and stride. If you interfere between the fences and restrict the horse, it will be your fault that the horse knocks them down and he will not learn from this.

SUMMARY

- Always start and finish a cross-country schooling session by jumping one or two straightforward fences such as a log and an ascending spread.
- When jumping a series of fences, a balanced, forward-going canter must be quickly re-established after each jump. Do not progress to jumping anything complicated until the horse feels confident over easy fences.
- Remember that it is always better to do a small amount, and to take home a confident horse which will approach the next training session with eagerness, than a horse whose confidence has been eroded by a bad jump.
- In the early stages of a horse's jumping career, he will benefit from a cross-country schooling session or a small competition every two weeks if possible.
- If you go to a competition at this stage, allow for the horse being unsettled by the noise, the other horses and the unfamiliar surroundings, and give yourself plenty of time to accustom him to these things before you start to warm him up. It is also important at this stage to choose a course that he can manage easily, to promote his and your confidence.

5

RIDING CROSS-COUNTRY FENCES

Cross-country riding can be split into many categories. The points to be taken into consideration are:

- the fences to be jumped
- the terrain to be crossed
- the going and the weather conditions
- the speed at which you are hoping to ride the course
- whether you are competing so that the horse can gain experience, or whether you hope to win

All these factors must in turn be related to the severity of the course and the experience of both you and the horse. This chapter describes in detail some of the fences that you will encounter on a cross-country course, and gives advice on how to negotiate them under a range of different circumstances.

Uprights

An upright is the term used for a vertical fence which has no spread. There are many variations, including posts and rails, sleepers, brick or stone walls, echelons, palisades, balustrades, stiles, Helsinki steps and gates (**fig. 38**). These are all upright fences, but the appearance of each can produce different reactions from the

horse, so you cannot approach them all in the same way.

For example, uprights which have daylight showing through them look more flimsy than their solid cousins, and need to be approached with a little more care, whereas the more solid uprights with no daylight between the structures give a horse much more to jump, and so he will often show greater respect for them. Although an accurate take-off is still required, be careful not to ride too cautiously to an upright fence, as the horse may back off and, if his canter lacks energy, he may come to a grinding halt in front of the fence before you have even noticed.

A balanced, rhythmical approach, without too much speed, is needed for an accurate take-off at an upright fence. As there is only height to jump, and not a spread, it does not matter if the horse jumps a little too deliberately. What is important is trying to find the correct speed from about twenty strides away, and then maintaining the rhythm and balance to the fence. A stile can be very narrow, so holding the horse on to a line is just as important here as an accurate take-off (**fig. 39**).

Helsinki steps are a little more technical, as they are still upright, but are built on the side of a hill or slope (**fig. 40**). It is

Fig. 38 Gates form the straightforward type of upright
fence frequently found on a cross-country course

Fig. 39 A stile can be very narrow and requires a
straight approach and accurate take-off

Fig. 40 Helsinki steps

imperative here that you are able to keep the horse on a line to the fence without him drifting off down the hill and past the fence. It is advisable to avoid jumping an outside rail as it may encourage the horse to run out, so try to jump one of the middle rails, and keep the horse on a slight uphill line so that he is not tempted to run out. Sometimes, due to the terrain, these fences can only be jumped in one place, in which case you have no choice, but make sure that you have planned your approach well. As with the other uprights, try to be very accurate by ensuring that the canter is of a good quality.

Ground lines

Ground lines are usually constructed either as a lower rail at ground level, set out a little from the top rail; or as a lower rail secured on dummy posts approximately halfway from the ground and the top rail, either in line with the top rail or set out a little **(fig. 41)**. The addition of a ground line makes the fence look more inviting, so that it is psychologically easier to approach from the rider's point of view. If the top rail is prominent, however, or the fence is leaning toward the take-off

side, a false ground line is created. Fence builders should avoid this situation as it draws the horse into the bottom of the fence, resulting in a take-off point too close to the fence, but this does sometimes occur and so you should be prepared.

An upright or vertical fence is the basis for many different fences. It can be quite difficult to judge the correct take-off point on the approach if there is no ground line, as a fence constructed only with a top rail can look very airy. Even a solid upright, such as a wall, can be difficult to judge when there is no ground line, as you can be drawn into the base of the fence, so it is useful to imagine a ground line, as this will help you to arrive at the correct take-off point **(fig. 42)**.

An accurate, rhythmical canter with the horse balanced between your hands and legs is the best way to approach an upright sited on level ground. This type of approach will help the horse to jump high enough over the fence, whereas an unbalanced, inaccurate take-off may result in the horse hitting the fence and then falling. It is important to practise riding to uprights of the same height that you will encounter in competitions, so that you learn to feel how the horse needs to approach in order to jump them successfully.

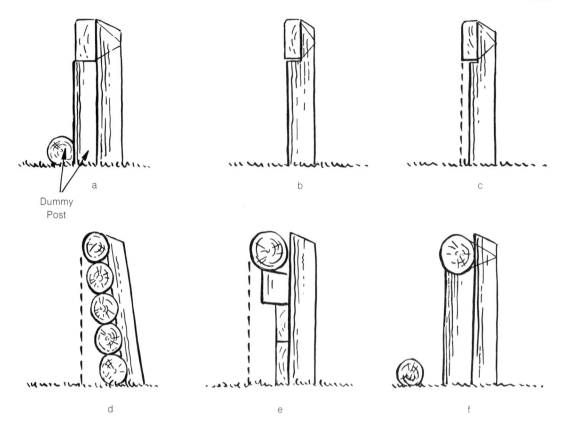

Fig. 41 Upright fences and ground lines

a An upright with a lower rail secured on dummy posts, giving a true ground line

b An upright fence with no ground line

c An upright with a prominent top rail, giving a false ground line

d An upright with a top rail leaning towards the take-off, giving a false ground line

e An upright with a top rail constructed of larger timber than that used for the bottom rail, giving a false ground line

f A ground line set out from the top rail, giving a true ground line

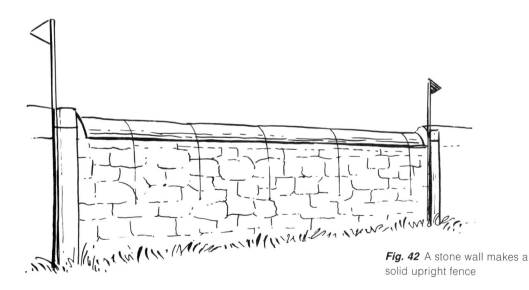

Fig. 42 A stone wall makes a solid upright fence

Uprights sited on difficult terrain (fig. 43)

A level take-off and landing before a downhill slope

The horse is able to take off and land over this fence before he has to adjust his balance for the downhill slope. However, the landing platform may be short, and the horse may not be able to see where he is going to land, so this fence will test his boldness. You must therefore give him confidence and ensure that he approaches the fence with a lot of contained energy and good balance. If he is going too fast he may become unbalanced on the landing side, or may even hit the fence with one or more legs as he tries to slow himself down in preparation for the downhill slope on landing.

You must keep a strong lower leg and under no circumstances get in front of the movement by letting your upper body tip forward, or you will not be able to drive the horse forward if he backs off the fence.

In addition, you will lose your balance and will be unable to help the horse if he hits the fence, or if he stumbles or becomes unbalanced on the landing side.

A downhill approach and landing

Here the horse can see where he is going, and where the landing is, so this

Fig. 43 Uprights sited on difficult terrain

a A level take-off and landing before a downhill slope

b A downhill approach and landing

c A level approach and downhill landing

d An uphill approach with a level or uphill landing

e Helsinki steps on the side of a hill

f An upright on level ground but with the ground dipping away on take-off

g Uprights at the bottom of a slope, with a level landing

   i the fence is positioned at the bottom of the slope

   ii the fence is positioned so that the horse has one stride on level ground before take-off

   iii the fence is positioned 1 to 1·5 m (3 to 5 ft) beyond the bottom of the slope

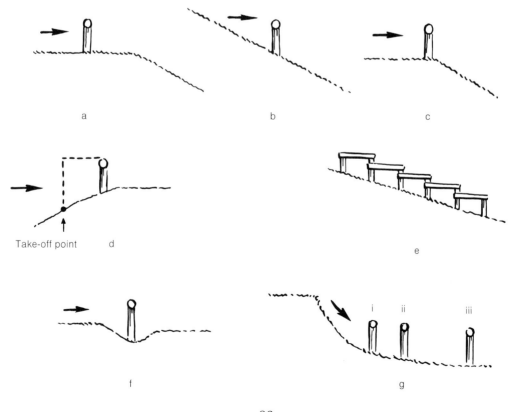

fence is relatively straightforward provided that:

- you keep the horse in balance with the weight off his forehand on the approach
- the horse does not over-jump the fence and land too steeply, causing a loss of balance which may result in a fall
- the approach is not too fast, as the horse will be out of balance on landing, which may cause him to fall
- the approach is not too slow and unenergetic, which may lead to the horse refusing due to lack of commitment
- you do not get in front of the movement and unbalance the horse

A level approach with a downhill landing The horse cannot see where he is going to land, so this type of fence tests boldness. It also demands athleticism, as, in addition to jumping the fence, the horse must be balanced in order to cope with the drop. An energetic, balanced canter is required on the approach, but without too much speed, as this would make it impossible for the horse to get his legs down quickly enough on landing.

Common mistakes are as follows:

- the horse slithers to a halt on take-off because you have failed to prepare the horse correctly and let your upper body get in front of the movement
- the horse takes off but leaves his forearms on the fence, which usually results in a fall
- the horse over-jumps the fence and either fails to land in balance, or lands too steeply and then pecks or stumbles
- the horse takes off too far away, and drags his hindlegs through the fence as he attempts to find ground to land on

If you feel that things are not going according to plan, you can save the horse from falling if you keep your upper body behind the movement and your lower legs forward, so that you are able to slip the reins if necessary and allow the horse freedom of his head and neck. At the same time, you can help to support the forehand by holding on to the reins and keeping your weight well back.

An uphill approach with a level or uphill landing The height of this fence is measured from the approximate take-off point. This means that the actual fence looks under-sized, which may lead to an indifferent jump. From the course builder's point of view, it is better to position this type of fence on the brow of a hill, so that the horse can take off on level ground, over a fence which looks more in proportion to the rest of the course. This is still a demanding test, as the horse has to climb the hill while maintaining sufficient impulsion to jump the fence.

To negotiate this type of fence correctly, the horse's hindlegs must be engaged on the approach, the impulsion must be maintained or increased if necessary in the final approach, and you must remain in balance and not get left behind, or you will be unable to use your seat and lower legs correctly to create and maintain the impulsion. You will also find it difficult to catch up with the movement once the horse has taken off. The take-off point must not be too far from the fence, or the horse will land 'flat' and in no position to jump another fence a stride or two later if required. Horses often land over these types of fences with little impulsion or forward movement, so you must anticipate this and use stronger aids on landing in order to maintain the energy created on the approach.

An upright on the side of a hill, e.g., Helsinki steps (see fig. 40 on page 84) Try to avoid jumping one of the outer steps, as this will leave no margin for error if the horse drifts. Decide on the best point to jump the fence when you walk the course, and, on the approach, focus your eye on that part of the fence. Approaching the steps on a slight uphill angle will lessen the chances of the horse running out. Keep him on the pre-planned line, and do not let him drift.

An upright on level ground, but where the ground dips away on take-off For this fence, it is important to maintain impulsion and to keep the horse off his forehand on the approach. If you do not do this, his attention may be taken by the dip, and if his impulsion fades and you tip forward, his forelegs will slide into the dip on the take-off side.

An upright at the bottom of a slope, with a level landing Here, it is important to consider the position of the fence in relation to the slope. There are three alternatives.

(a) The fence may be positioned at the bottom of the slope, so that the horse takes off from the slope and lands on level ground. As the horse has pushed off from the slope, he is in effect jumping from higher to lower ground, which may be a little punishing when his forelegs meet the ground on landing.

(b) The fence may be positioned so that the horse has one stride on level ground before he takes off, allowing him to negotiate the slope and then to prepare for the fence. This makes the jump easier than (a), as long as the horse does not dive off the slope and throw himself at the fence, only to find that he has left himself no room in which to re-balance himself before jumping the vertical.

This type of fence is a real test of your balance and feel for the horse, because any unnecessary movement may unbalance him. Learning to sit and wait for the horse to take off,

instead of trying to tell him what to do by throwing your upper body forward or by giving him a big kick when you think it is time to jump, is a skill that must be learned if these fences are to be negotiated successfully.

(c) The fence may be positioned 1 to 1·5 metres (3 to 5 ft) beyond the bottom of the slope. The take-off for this fence is very difficult, as the actual placing of the horse's front feet, as he descends the slope, is very hard to judge and control. A take-off position from the slope would require a huge effort from the horse, resulting in an unbalanced landing, so a controlled descent of the slope is needed so that the horse can jump from the level ground.

Spreads

A spread fence is any fence other than an upright or vertical, at which the horse has to jump both height and width. The spread part of the fence can comprise straw bales, barrels, sleepers, ditches, tyres or hedges. The important point when jumping spreads is to ensure that the horse has enough energy within the pace from which to jump the height and clear the spread. There are many differing ways of presenting a spread fence, and some ask more demanding questions from the horse and rider than others.

Ascending spreads

Provided that the approach, take-off, landing and getaway are all on level ground, this is the easiest type of spread fence **(fig. 44)**.

● The shape of the fence helps both you and the horse to judge the correct take-off point. The horse does not have to reach the highest part of his jump until

Fig. 44 An ascending spread constructed of wooden sleepers makes an inviting fence and provides a natural take-off point

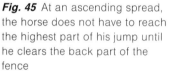

Fig. 45 At an ascending spread, the horse does not have to reach the highest part of his jump until he clears the back part of the fence

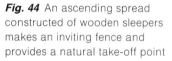

he is clearing the back part of the fence, making it difficult to take off too close **(fig. 45)**. If he takes off too far away, as long as he has sufficient impulsion and the spread is no more than 1 metre (3 ft), he will compensate by jumping with a bigger, longer arc than he would need for a take-off point closer to the fence.

- An accurate, balanced approach is less important than for other fences, so if impulsion is lacking or the speed is not quite correct, it is still possible for the horse to jump the fence well.

- An ascending spread is not demanding in terms of boldness and honesty. There are no ditches or elements to frighten the horse, so an ascending spread with straightforward dimensions is a good fence from which both young and old horses can gain confidence. This fence

is also ideal when introducing cross-country fences to horses which have just begun to canter to their fences.

Square, true or box parallels

These types of fences are quite difficult to jump, especially when they are constructed to the maximum dimensions allowed for a particular competition, and when the siting incorporates other factors. In contrast to the jump needed for an ascending spread, the horse must reach sufficient height in the first part of the arc in order to clear the first or front rail, before opening up the arc to clear the spread **(fig. 46)**.

When considering the siting of a true parallel, the same approaches apply as to the siting of an upright. If a horse takes off

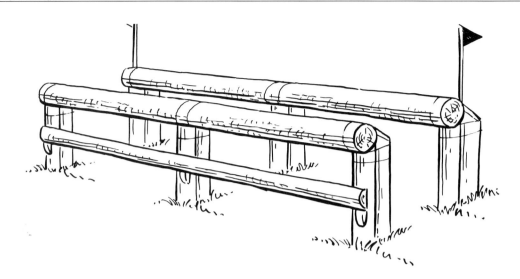

Fig. 46 Square, true or box parallels

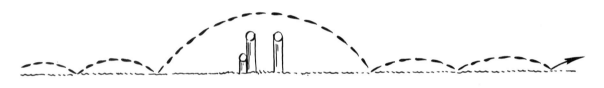

Fig. 47 Strides should not be 'taken out' when jumping a spread fence such as a parallel, or the jump will be long and flat, resulting in a long, flat canter on the landing side

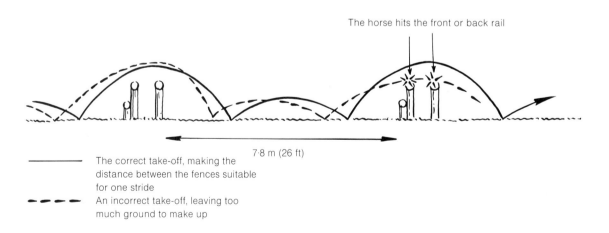

The horse hits the front or back rail

7·8 m (26 ft)

—————— The correct take-off, making the distance between the fences suitable for one stride

- - - - - An incorrect take-off, leaving too much ground to make up

Fig. 48 If too few strides are taken and a parallel is the first part of a combination, the horse will land short and have to make up too much distance before the next fence, especially if this is also a parallel

too far away from an upright, however, he has only the height to worry about, whereas if the majority of the jump is used in making the distance from take-off to the front rail of a parallel, he may have to stretch to reach the back rail. On landing, the horse will be unbalanced, and so the canter must be re-established before the next fence. It is therefore important not to 'lose' strides when jumping fences in quick succession – especially spreads – for several reasons:

- the horse has to make an unnecessary effort to clear the back rail
- the jump will be long and flat, resulting in a long, flat canter on the landing side **(fig. 47)**
- if the spread is very wide, the horse may not be able to clear it with his hindlegs, as his forelegs may only just reach to the landing side
- if the parallel is the first part of a combination, the horse will not land far enough over it and there will be too much distance to make up between the fences **(fig. 48)**

It is important that the back rail of a parallel is visible and not concealed either by a front rail or a hedge **(fig. 49)**. It is also inadvisable to jump a parallel with a false ground line, because the horse will be drawn to the base of the fence and choose a take-off point that is too close to the front rail. This may cause him to hit the front rail, making it virtually impossible to clear the back rail as all forward motion and balance will be lost. The result could

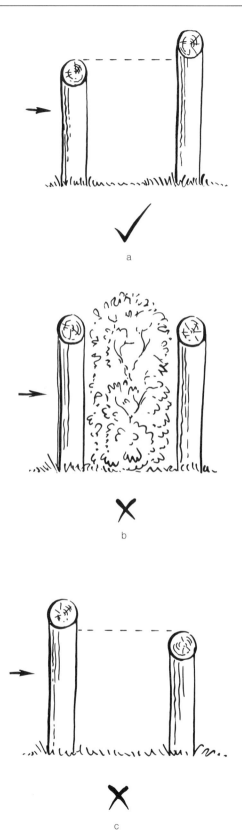

Fig. 49 The back rail of a parallel must be visible
a   The back rail is higher than the front rail, and is therefore visible
b   The back rail is obscured by a hedge
c   The back rail is invisible because it is lower than the front rail

be very unpleasant, causing a loss of confidence to both horse and rider, not to mention injury.

A hayrack standing on its own provides a false ground line (fig. 50). This type of fence is best avoided for novice or preliminary-level horses unless the take-off side has a true ground line such as bales or sleepers.

A large spread with a considerable drop on the landing side can prove very difficult (fig. 51). A horse will prepare himself for a lower landing, minimizing the drop by lowering his undercarriage as soon as possible after taking off. If he misjudges the width of the fence he may lower his undercarriage too quickly, landing either on the back rail or dropping short between the rails. If this type of fence is to be safe, the spread should be reasonable, but not of maximum proportions, and the severity of the drop should not be too demanding or punishing. A collected pace with plenty of

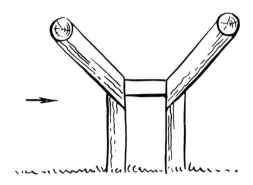

Fig. 50 A hayrack standing on its own gives a false ground line

impulsion is of great importance when approaching a fence of this nature, as, if the horse is travelling too fast, he may lose his balance on the landing side and fall.

Ditches

Sloping rails constructed over a ditch make a relatively easy fence, because the

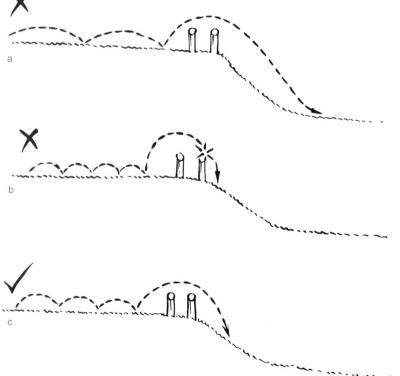

Fig. 51 **A spread with a drop on landing**
a The strides are too long and flat. The horse may lose his balance on the landing side and fall
b The approach strides are too short. The jump is too high, and may not be wide enough
c The correct approach. The strides are even, the jump is neither too high nor too wide and the horse should land in balance

Fig. 52 Sloping rails over a ditch

28 Sloping rails over a ditch. This young horse has veered to the left and is jumping the fence on the extreme left. The take-off is a little unbalanced and the forelegs are not a pair, indicating lack of confidence. The rider's lower legs have slipped back and her upper body has come a little too far forward

rails form an ascending spread and this is the easiest type of fence to judge and jump (**fig. 52**). As long as the lowest rail is fairly close to the ground and the timber is of substantial proportions, the majority of the ditch is covered up and the horse has no idea that there is a ditch there at all.

You should approach this fence with plenty of impulsion, so that if the horse backs off a little he will still have enough energy to jump. A half-hearted approach which lacks impulsion could result in a refusal, as, if the horse hesitates and you are not quick enough to use your seat and legs to drive him forward, he will run out of impulsion and will be unable to jump the fence. It is important to negotiate this type of fence with a minimum of effort and fuss, so that the horse gains the maximum confidence with which to negotiate the more complex ditch-related fences (**28–30**).

A ditch on the take-off side

This type of ditch provides a large, dark hole, and usually makes the fence fairly wide. The more substantial the fence, the more the horse's eye can be drawn away from the ditch, but the wider, deeper and darker the ditch (with little or no ground line), the more the horse's eye will be drawn into it. Once he catches sight of the ditch, his neck will tend to get longer and lower, which in turn places more weight on the forehand. If you are then pulled forward over the horse's withers, your position will be weakened, making it difficult for you to use your seat and legs to drive the horse forward.

If the horse backs off the fence on the approach, and you are not quick enough to regain the impulsion, there is no altern-

29 The horse's forelegs have still not quite come together as a pair. The rider has opened her fingers to allow him to use his head and neck – she has probably had to do this as her lower legs have slipped back and her hips are behind the movement. The horse appears confident, but the rider is looking down and looks as though she will be glad to get to the other side

ative but for the horse to refuse. A real problem can then begin if the combined spread of the ditch and the height of the fence is considerable. Once a horse has stopped at a large ditch and looked into the bottom of it, he can lose confidence, which can make it virtually impossible to persuade him to jump it at all. It is therefore vital to ensure that:

• the horse has been schooled over dry and water ditches
• the horse jumps these ditches with maximum confidence
• the size of ditch encountered in competition is comparable with the horse's stage of training
• you always approach ditch fences with the horse in balance, straight and with plenty of impulsion, and that you are in a position from which you can drive the horse forward
• you always have a positive, forward-thinking attitude which will give the horse confidence

If you adhere to all these points, the horse need never know that there is a dark, deep ditch on the take-off side and therefore will never lose confidence.

30 The horse and rider look much more purposeful the next time. The horse's forelegs are together and the jump appears straighter. The rider's lower legs have slipped back again and her hands have gone forward towards the ears instead of the mouth, but she is looking straight ahead and seems to have greater confidence in this jump

A ditch on the landing side

This type of ditch is often 'blind', when the fence is solid and hides the ditch. As long as the ditch, or fence and ditch combined, is not unduly wide, the horse will not be perturbed, but if he lands short over the fence, he may easily land in the ditch **(fig. 53)**. To avoid this possibility, you must ensure that the horse has a positive

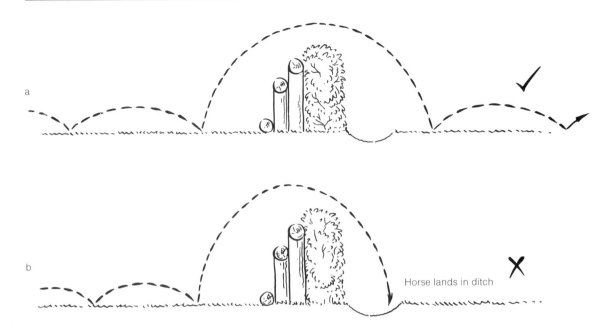

approach, and that the pace has plenty of impulsion. If combined with an accurate approach, this will ensure that the ditch is of no consequence.

When a ditch is positioned on the landing side of a post-and-rail fence, it becomes visible, especially if the post and rail is made of insubstantial timber. This can draw the horse's eye into the base of the fence, making it difficult for him to judge the correct take-off position. In effect, the ditch creates a false ground line. This type of fence can often trick horses, so particular care should be taken on the approach to prepare the horse so that he has the best chance of negotiating the ditch successfully.

Trakheners

This type of fence consists of a substantial pole or log placed over a ditch. The degree of difficulty of a trakhener depends on the following factors.

- The siting of the fence. If there is a downhill approach, the horse may fall

Fig. 53 A ditch on the landing side
a The correct approach
b An incorrect approach. If the horse lands short over the fence, he may well land in the ditch

on to his forehand, and his eye may be drawn from the log or rail and into the ditch, making the fence a real test of boldness and confidence.
- The dimensions of the ditch. The wider, deeper and darker this is, the more confident the horse needs to be. A natural dry ditch which is grassed over is the easiest type of ditch for a horse to jump, whereas a sleepered ditch which resembles a black hole is a greater test of boldness and confidence because it draws the horse's eye to it.
- The thickness of the log or rail. The more substantial this is, the easier the fence will be, as the horse will keep focusing on this instead of the ditch.
- The placing of the log or rail in relation to the ditch. If the rail is placed across the ditch, you have a choice of take-off positions **(fig. 54)**. The best place to jump the fence is where the ditch is

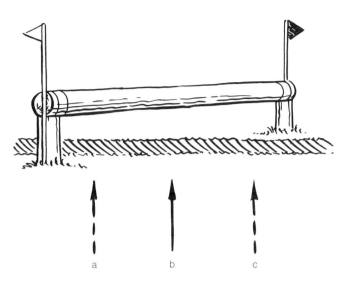

Fig. 54 A trakhener
a Here there is too much ditch on the landing side
b This is the correct place to jump. The ditch is slightly in front of the rail and therefore acts as a ground line
c Here there is too much ditch on the take-off side

a   b   c

slightly in front of the rail and therefore acts as a ground line **(31–5)**. If the rail is positioned immediately above the front facing of the ditch, a more difficult situation is produced because the ditch creates a false ground line. If, as a result, the horse misjudges the take-off point and is too close to the fence, he will be unable to raise his forehand high enough to avoid hitting the fence. This type of fence provides a very difficult challenge, and should only be used to test the accuracy and boldness of a very experienced horse.

If the rail is positioned to the rear of the ditch, the front of the ditch will provide a good ground line which will help you to present the horse accurately at the fence. At the same time, a positive, balanced, forward-thinking approach, with your eyes looking ahead and not in the ditch, is necessary to produce a confident jump.

Brush or birch fences

These fences are usually constructed in the shape of an ascending spread, which makes them relatively easy to jump. As with most things in life, however, they still have their pitfalls. They can look very black and imposing, which encourages the less-experienced horse to back off. This means that the fence must be approached with plenty of impulsion, and you must keep your leg on to keep the horse going forward.

As brush or birch fences are ascending spreads without a rail at the highest point, they do not require a great deal of accuracy, but it is bad discipline and training to let the horse fall through them or take off too early and drag his hindlegs through them. They should be jumped from a rhythmic canter and with the same concentration that you would give to a more complex fence. If the horse over-jumps at first, do not worry, as he will jump more smoothly as he becomes more confident.

Brush fences with ditches on take-off

These ditches usually have a good guard rail, so there should be no doubt in your mind as to where the ditch starts **(fig. 55)**. The ditch increases the width of the spread, so it is ideal to ride to a take-off point close to the ditch (a similar approach is used when jumping a triple bar in show jumping). Problems arise when the horse gallops at the brush fence regardless of the

31 (*Top left*) The young horse is backing off the trakhener, with a low forehand and long neck. He has pulled the rider's upper body and arms forward, and her lower legs have slipped back. As a result, she is out of balance and cannot stop the horse from slowing down and dropping further on to his forehand. The hindlegs have almost come to a standstill and are digging into the ground

32 (*Bottom left*) The rider has regained a secure lower-leg position, but the horse is now so intent on looking in the ditch that the rider is in a hopeless situation

33 (*Above*) The horse now thinks that the easy way out is to run through his left shoulder. The rider tries desperately to stop him by using the outside leg and the inside rein, but the horse has so much right neck bend that there will be a lot of weight on the left shoulder, making it difficult to stop him from running left

ditch, as he will then miss his stride because he is going too fast, and will be out of balance. He may gallop straight through the fence, or fall, or produce a very untidy jump which will break the rhythm so that he loses all forward momentum on the landing side.

If the horse backs off the fence, leaving him with insufficient impulsion with which to jump it, he may fall into the ditch, refuse or produce an uncomfortable 'bunny-hop' jump which will leave him with no impulsion on the landing side. If you think your horse may back off, always approach the fence with plenty of impulsion. If you begin to feel him backing off, drive him forward with your seat and legs, and use the whip to back up your leg aids if necessary. The key to jumping this fence – as with many other cross-country fences – is to act sooner rather than later in order to avoid a refusal.

34 The horse tries another tactic – rearing up and swivelling round on his hindlegs. In this situation the rider has to react very quickly and get her weight and hands forward, or she runs the risk of pulling the horse over backward. The horse may also lose his own balance and topple over either sideways or backward

35 Eventually the horse jumps the fence in rather an exaggerated and unbalanced way. The rider is doing her best to anchor her lower legs, while allowing the horse the freedom of his head and neck

Other types of brush or birch fences

Birch is sometimes added to a wooden frame to make an upright fence. This needs to be ridden accurately because it is upright, although it is a more forgiving fence than a post and rail because there is only birch if the horse hits the top. Do not encourage bad jumping by thinking that the fence is forgiving, however, or one day the horse may not achieve enough height with a lazy jump, and then he will fall. Horses usually respect this type of fence because it looks dark and rather ominous,

but often back off because they are nervous of the unseen landing. Information on riding a birch fence as part of a coffin can be found on page 111.

Bullfinches

A bullfinch is basically a brush fence with a thin network of branches protruding vertically from the top of the fence, through which the horse jumps. The severity of a bullfinch is determined by the height and thickness of the network of branches, and the spread of the fence **(fig. 56)**. The most difficult arrangement is a parallel of birch fences with a thick, high bullfinch on the far fence, so that the horse has to jump the spread of the parallel and then the height of the bullfinch.

The approach to a fence of this kind must be balanced and straight. The canter must be strong with lots of impulsion, and

Fig. 55 There is usually a substantial guard rail in front of a brush or birch fence, which makes the start of the ditch obvious

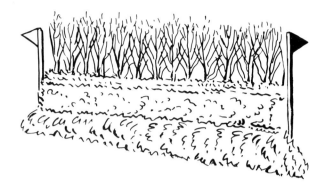

Fig. 56 The severity of a bullfinch depends on its height, spread and the thickness of the branches

the horse should be going forward into your hands so that you feel that he has plenty of stored power. An accurate take-off position is also important, as there is both a spread and height to jump. If the take-off is too far away, the horse may straddle the back part of the fence. You should have a secure position in the saddle with strong lower legs, and, by staying close to the horse with your upper body, you will be in an ideal position to absorb the inevitably big jump. Even small bull-finches may result in a huge jump from the horse, so do not get caught out! See page 111 for information on riding a bullfinch-type fence as part of a coffin.

Hedges

Hedges on their own do not jump very well, so they are usually padded out by the introduction of a ground rail, a ground and a top rail, or a back rail. The rails must not be introduced in such a way as to make the fence unsafe: if a top rail is used, it must be backed up with a true or promi-nent rail either at ground level or sup-ported with a rail 10 to 20 centimetres (6 to 16 ins) from ground level. If it is on the take-off side, the top rail must not be more prominent than the height of the hedge. If a back rail is used, it must be visible from the take-off side. It is acceptable to place a rail on top of the hedge, as long as this does not create a false ground line.

Overhead obstructions

A roof or railed arch may be constructed over a fence, and, as long as this is high enough above the fence, it should not cause any problems. Do not attempt to jump a fence of this nature unless the overhead construction is more than 3·3 metres (11 ft) above it. Horses may back off because they are unsure of the nature of the fence, so a controlled, balanced, straight approach is necessary. This will ensure that, if the horse baulks a little, he will still have the confidence to keep going forward if you encourage him to do so by using your legs.

Coffins

A coffin fence consists of three elements: the first fence (usually a rail), a ditch and another fence. This is a fence found on the majority of cross-country courses, and it is used to test your ability to approach in balance, with sufficient impulsion and at the correct speed. It also tests the horse's boldness, agility and confidence. The degree of difficulty of a coffin is dictated by:

- the siting of the fence
- the steepness of the slope on either side of the ditch
- the distance between the rails and the ditch

- the dimensions of the ditch
- the height of the rails
- the state of the going
- the use of materials other than rails

It is vital that a coffin has been introduced to the horse prior to his first competition, ideally in a schooling situation. The horse must first jump the ditch with confidence. A rail one or two strides after the ditch can then be introduced, and the horse jumps the rail as a progression from the ditch. Once the horse has mastered the ditch and rail, another rail can be introduced as the first element of the coffin.

At this stage, the dimensions of the rails and the ditch should be kept simple: the rails should be around 80 centimetres ($2\frac{3}{4}$ ft) and the ditch no wider than 60 centimetres (2 ft) wide. The distances between the elements should not trick the horse: ideally they should be between 5·4 and 6·3 metres (18 to 21 ft) for one stride; and 9 and 10·5 metres (30 to 33 ft) for two strides. Incorrect or unfair distances will confuse the horse, as each part of the coffin will not come as a natural progression from the

previous one; whereas if he is able to land over each part and then take one or two even strides, he will soon be jumping smoothly through the coffin. The easiest type of coffin is sited on level ground, with the first rail at a height that encourages the horse to jump, and a ditch that is not too dark, deep or wide. The further the ditch is from the first rail, the less influence it has on the rail (**fig. 57**).

The approach to a coffin is very important, because the whole fence needs to be considered. The horse must be in balance and straight on the approach, and his speed must be adequate. If it is too slow, he may refuse at the first or succeeding elements, or may not have enough impulsion to carry him through all the elements. In this case, he may jump very laboriously and hit the final rail. If the approach is too fast, the horse will find it difficult to balance himself sufficiently to jump all the elements, which come in quick succession. In addition, the strides will be too long and will cover too much ground, making it difficult for the horse to find enough room between each element (**fig. 58**).

Fig. 57 A coffin sited on level ground with a low first rail is a relatively easy fence

Fig. 58 If the approach to a coffin is too fast, the horse will be unable to retain his balance over all the elements, particularly if the distances are tight

Horse lands too far out and falls in ditch

POINTS TO REMEMBER

A coffin is difficult when:

- the going is slippery
- the approach is downhill
- the first rail is upright and the maximum height allowed for the competition
- the slopes on either side of the ditch are severe and the distances tight (fig. 59)
- the ditch is very wide and/or deep
- the second rail is of maximum height

If the approach is downhill, the horse will need a canter that is full of contained energy. This will ensure that he is going forward from your legs into your hands, and that his stride is of a suitable length to cope with the short distances in the coffin. His forehand will also be light, enabling him to make enough height over the first rail. You must keep a strong lower-leg position on the approach so that you can drive the horse forward by activating the hindquarters if you feel that the canter is fading. You must also sit up and keep your shoulders back, so that there is no danger of your getting in front of the movement or being pitched forward if the horse hits the first rail.

Ideally, the first rail should be jumped from a balanced canter. Allow the horse to use his head and neck by offering the rein forward toward the horse's mouth so that he determines how much he takes the rein, but do not lose the contact, throw your upper body forward or let your lower legs slide backward. On a downhill approach to the first rail or the ditch, it is of the utmost importance that you keep your lower-leg position vertical with the weight in your heels, so that you can help the horse if he backs off or lands awkwardly over the first rail.

The ditch should be jumped economically if the landing is steep, or you may find that the horse has jumped into the bank, making it very difficult to create enough energy to jump the last rail. Jumping the ditch too extravagantly may also make it impossible for the horse to take a stride before the last element, as he will have made up too much ground and there will be insufficient room between his landing position and the next take-off point.

You must try to stay in balance throughout, and judge how much rein the horse requires over each element. You must sit still over the ditch so that the horse is not encouraged to over-jump, keeping your lower legs on in case the horse backs off the ditch or lacks energy. Try not to get in front of or behind the movement on the slope up to the final element, as this will unbalance the horse, causing an untidy or awkward jump. It is important to keep the horse straight throughout the whole coffin, or you may find that he drifts past the ditch or the last rail. The straighter the horse, the easier it is for him to remain in good balance, and therefore to jump correctly (36–41).

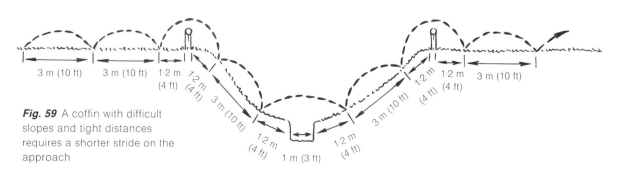

3 m (10 ft) 3 m (10 ft) 1·2 m (4 ft) 1·2 m (4 ft) 3 m (10 ft) 1·2 m (4 ft) 1 m (3 ft) 1·2 m (4 ft) 3 m (10 ft) 1·2 m (4 ft) 1·2 m (4 ft) 3 m (10 ft)

Fig. 59 A coffin with difficult slopes and tight distances requires a shorter stride on the approach

36 The horse has made a clean jump over the first element of the coffin, although he is slightly right of centre. Both he and the rider are in balance. The rider's upper body is in a good position, ready to drive the horse over the ditch, and the lower legs are forward. Perfect!

37 The horse has started to back off the ditch, and is drifting to the left. He is thinking of a way to avoid jumping the ditch, but the rider is determined to keep driving him forward so that he cannot stop or run out

38 As he has started to drift to the left, the horse has started to become unbalanced as he prepares to take off over the ditch

39 The jump over the ditch is very unbalanced and deliberate – showing lack of confidence – and the rider has become slightly unbalanced because of the big and crooked jump

40 The landing is remarkably good, and both horse and rider are regaining their balance. The horse is concentrating on the rail and the rider looks determined to make the jump over it more comfortable than the jump over the ditch. The rider's hands are a little high, and the reins are a little long

41 The horse makes a clean, reasonably balanced jump at the final element, although his forelegs are not a pair. The rider's hands are towards the ears rather than the mouth, and the reins are a little loose – probably as a result of the way the horse jumped the ditch. This is not a problem here, as the landing is level and this is the final part of the combination. The rider has come rather high out of the saddle and her lower legs have slipped back again

Lastly, when walking a cross-country course, try to find a line at the coffin where:

- the ground is good (if it is slippery or poached, find the best area that you can)
- the slopes are at their most gradual
- at the first element, the landing side drops away the least
- at the last element, the take-off point is as level as possible

Birch fences

These can replace each of the rails at a coffin, making the slope and ditch on the landing side of the first element invisible as the horse is approaching. The sloping nature of the birch will encourage you to approach more positively whereas a post and rail, being less forgiving, requires more accurate riding and may therefore make you approach a little tentatively and over-cautiously. A birch fence as the third element is always kinder than a rail, but be sure to ride positively in case the horse backs off or jumps very big.

There is also a tendency to jump birch fences too freely. Be careful not to make this mistake, as the horse will be travelling too quickly for a safe negotiation of the ditch and final element.

Bullfinch-type fences

As has already been discussed on page 101, a horse usually jumps very high over bullfinches, so the danger lies when he lands very steeply on the downhill slope of a coffin fence. As with a birch fence, a bullfinch hides the ditch and third element, but it also presents other problems. The horse normally lowers his undercarriage in preparation for a lower landing, but is unable to do so when jumping this high. When a horse lands very steeply, he has a lot of weight on his forehand. If the

slope is steep and the distance to the ditch short, he may therefore be unable to take off over the ditch. If the horse falls into the ditch, you will be left with a three-fold problem:

- the horse will have had a nasty fright
- he will be wary of jumping another bullfinch
- he will lack confidence at the next coffin he approaches

If a bullfinch is used as the first element of a coffin, it should be kept to a reasonable height and density in order to avoid this situation. It is also inadvisable to have a high, dense bullfinch at the third element, because the horse must jump very high but not wide if he is to clear it. In this case, it is vital that your take-off point is not too far away. If you do attempt to take off too far away, the horse will only be able to produce a flat, low jump and will not make the height, because the first part of his jump will have been used to make up the ground lost through the incorrect take-off position. Another potential problem with a high bullfinch at the third element is that, if the horse has scrambled over the ditch, he may land out of balance with no impulsion from which to produce a jump with enough height.

Steps

Simple steps should have been included in your cross-country schooling sessions (see page 79) as a series of both uphill and downhill steps are often included in a course.

Downhill steps

Start with a single step. Approach either in a collected, forward-thinking canter, or in trot, depending on your horse's stage of training. The horse must be balanced, straight and listening to you. At the edge of the step, allow the horse to stretch his head and neck, but keep the contact and do not allow your upper body to be pulled forward or your lower legs to swing back. Ideally, your lower legs should be pushed slightly forward of the vertical with the weight remaining in your heels. The horse may land on all four feet at once, which can be disconcerting, but when he gets more confident he will jump more smoothly. The step should not be too narrow (less than 2·7 metres [9 ft]) or too high (over 90 centimetres [3 ft]) and the take-off and landing should be firm and level **(fig. 60)**.

Once the horse is confidently jumping down one step, introduce a second and then a third. Do not hurry him off the first step, as he will need to re-balance himself before the next one. Keep him straight and look ahead, but do not get pulled forward or you will be unable to keep him straight, balanced and going forwards.

Uphill steps

Start with a single step and keep to the same dimensions as for jumping steps downhill. The horse must be balanced and straight, and the approach should be in a collected, forward-thinking canter with your weight lightly in the saddle. Try to ride to an accurate take-off point, as for

jumping uprights **(fig. 61)**. If you choose a take-off point that is too far away, the horse will land flat, unbalanced and without impulsion; too close a take-off point will mean that he has to get his forehand out of the way of the face of the step very quickly, which can result in an unbalanced landing and the horse having an unpleasant feeling.

Keep a strong lower leg with a light seat, towards the back of the saddle. Keep your shoulders a little further forward than when jumping an upright to lessen the chance of being left behind. On take-off, think of jumping up the step, and allow the horse to use his head and neck by offering the rein forward, but without dropping the contact. When the horse is confident, introduce a second and then a third step. Approach the steps as before, but, on landing over the first step, drive the horse forward with your lower legs, keeping your upper body slightly forward so that you do not get behind the movement. If you are accurate at the first step, the horse should maintain the momentum all the way to the top, so try and land in the correct place each time so that he does not struggle to make the remaining steps. The steeper the steps, the more effort is required, so an accurate approach will help the horse.

The distances between steps often leave you feeling uncertain as to whether the

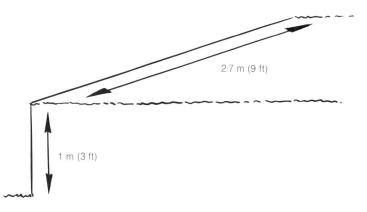

Fig. 60 Steps should not be too narrow or too high if they are to be negotiated safely

2·7 m (9 ft)

1 m (3 ft)

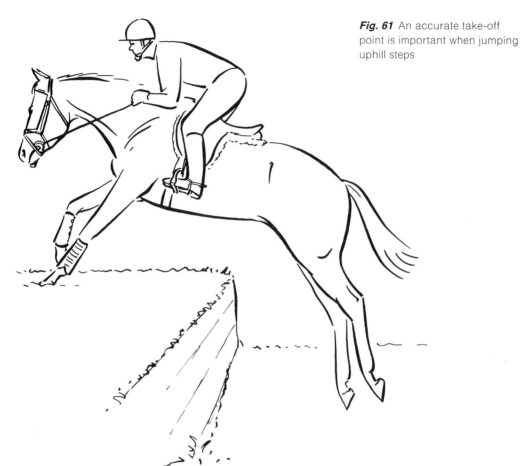

Fig. 61 An accurate take-off point is important when jumping uphill steps

horse is going to bounce them or put in a stride. The important thing in this situation is to make certain that the approach is balanced and straight, and that the horse has sufficient impulsion. Then, assuming that you stay in balance and do not hinder the horse, he will make up his own mind as to what is best. Problems will arise if you start to predict the horse's moment of take-off by throwing your upper body forward. As is the case with many types of fences, this will never help the horse to jump – all it will do is put the weight on his forehand, unbalance him and interrupt his concentration.

Sunken roads

This fence combines posts and rails with steps **(fig. 62)**. It tests the horse's boldness,

athleticism and ability to think quickly. The most straightforward type of sunken road with level ground consists of a post and rail, one stride to a step down, one or two strides to a step up, and one stride to a second post and rail.

When introducing the young horse to this type of fence, it is advisable to take it step by step. Practise jumping down and up the step, and, when the horse is confident, jump up the step and continue over the post and rail. The first rail should not be more than about 80 cm (30 in) at this stage. If all goes well, proceed to jumping the step down, followed by the step up and the post and rail as before. Finally, introduce the first rail and then proceed through the rest of the sunken road. By introducing the horse separately to each element in this way, he will understand the natural progression from one element to another and will negotiate the fence with confidence.

Riding into a sunken road

The approach to the first post and rail at a sunken road requires an approach similar that at the first element of a coffin. The horse must be balanced, straight, and attentive, with the canter containing plenty of energy but not too much speed, or he will be unable to keep his balance as he jumps through each element. The horse must be travelling forward in front of your legs so that you feel that he has an active, energetic canter which is available for use at any given time.

The more accurate your approach to the rail, the more easily the horse will jump through the elements. A take-off point which is too far away from the rail will result in the horse landing with his weight on his forehand and unbalanced. His out-line and steps, instead of being contained and energetic, will be long and flat. From here, having lost his balance and the quality of the canter, he may fall down the step. A take-off that is too close to the fence may result in the horse leaving one or both forearms on the top rail. From here, he may fall, or may scramble over the fence with you becoming unstable and therefore of no help to him on the landing side.

The step should be ridden as a downhill step (see page 111). You must be sure to stay in balance, and maintain contact with the reins, or it will be difficult to guide the horse through the remainder of the fence. The distance across the bottom of the road will determine how many strides to take: a distance of 5·4 to 6·6 metres (18 to 20 ft) is ideal for one stride, while 10 to 10·5 metres (33 to 35 ft) is ideal for two strides. A shorter distance is preferable to a longer distance, as an accurate take-off for the step up will help to produce a better jump over the second rail.

If the uphill step is going to come very quickly and the horse is likely to make up too much ground across the road, sit up and keep your shoulders up so that the horse is able to shorten his stride length and outline and to arrive at the step in a better position. If the distance between the two steps appears to be long, keep a strong leg when jumping down the first step so that the horse is encouraged to land further out into the road. On landing, driving the horse forward with your seat, back and legs so that you open up the stride and the horse makes up more ground. In this way he will reach a more suitable take-off position, from which he can negotiate the step up more easily. Your aim should be to jump the step up with purpose, not by the horse struggling laboriously, or the final element will prove very difficult.

To obtain an efficient jump at the step, you must feel that the horse is going forward into your hands, and that the canter still feels energetic. If this is not the case and the canter is diminishing, use your legs and the whip behind your leg if necessary to create more energy. It is of no

Fig. 62 A sunken-road fence comprises post-and-rail fences and steps

use to the horse if you tip forward in an attempt to create more energy, and this will only put additional weight on the forehand and make the canter even more laborious. The energy must be created in the hindquarters, and, as has been demonstrated in the early training exercises on the flat in Chapter One, the only way to achieve this is to use your legs and then to contain the energy by holding it with your seat and hands so that it can be released to jump up the step and then the final rail.

If the horse lands rather flat after the step up, it can be very difficult for the strides to cover the necessary amount of ground because he has lost his forward momentum. In this situation, it is sometimes safer to sit up, using your legs and seat to regain the lost energy and to collect and re-balance the horse, rather than trying to throw the horse at the fence with no impulsion and very little balance. Two or three short, active strides are often better than one or two long, flat unenergetic steps; the former provide the horse with the balance and the energy to jump the rail, whereas the latter may result in him falling over the rail because he does not have the energy or engagement necessary to jump the rail.

There is also the danger of your failing to realize that things are going wrong, and committing yourself to the fence by throwing your upper body forward when you think the horse should take off. This throws more weight on to the forehand, and, if the horse does not choose to take off at the same time, you cannot help him because you have already thrown his weight forward and your lower legs are ineffective, so that you have become a hindrance instead of a help.

POINTS TO REMEMBER

The difficulty of a sunken road depends on the following factors:

- the siting: e.g., there may be a change of light, or an uphill, downhill or undulating approach
- the height and positioning of the rails: these are sometimes set at an angle to the road crossing, or the rails could be arrowheads
- the distance between the rails and the steps
- the height of the steps and the distance between them
- the state of the going: if it gets badly poached, the horse will not get the same grip as with good going. On take-off ground may also be 'holding', making it more difficult for the horse to achieve enough lift from the ground
- a very difficult crossing would consist of: an approach into changing light; post-and-rail fences of maximum height; and tight distances (e.g., 2 to 3 metres [7 to 10 ft]) between each element. A fence of this complexity would only be suitable for experienced horses

Quarries

These usually comprise two or more fences strategically placed in and around a quarry-type site. The fences are often very solid, for example stone walls, big rails or sleepers. A basic quarry has an approach fence with a downhill landing. This requires boldness and athleticism, as the solid nature of the fence does not warn the horse of the drop and he does not see the lower landing until the last minute. If the fence is imposing, you must drive the horse forward in a positive approach. An athletic, balanced jump is ideal, as the horse will then land in a balanced way (**fig. 63**). To achieve this, an energetic canter with plenty of impulsion is more suitable than a faster canter, as the horse may fall on the landing side if the approach is too fast.

The exit fence often lies at the top of an uphill slope. It is important to keep the impulsion and balance up the hill, with the horse straight so that the fence comes easily to him. This is especially important if the exit fence has a big spread. If this is the case, an accurate take-off will allow the horse to incorporate the spread easily within the jump. If the take-off is too far away, however, he will waste most of his jump by having to make up the ground between the take-off point and the fence. He may then have to reach for the spread, which will result in an unbalanced landing.

Banks

The severity of a bank is determined by the amount of room on top of it, and by whether the sides are straight or sloping.

Fig. 63 An energetic, balanced canter is needed at a quarry so that the horse jumps and lands in balance

The more room there is on top of the bank, the easier it is to jump on and off, as there is more time for you and the horse to prepare yourselves for jumping off **(42–5)**. The less room there is, the more accurate your approach must be, because your landing on top must be balanced so that the horse can jump off immediately if necessary. Jumping a straight-sided bank is similar to jumping steps (see page 111).

Sometimes there is a rail on top of the bank. In this case, you must judge the approach to the step up on to the bank, so that the distance is correct from your landing point on the bank to the take-off point for the rail on top. A rail can be constructed at the far edge of the bank, so that the horse has to jump the rail and cope with the considerable drop on the other side. It is vital for this type of fence that the horse remains straight and in good balance, with plenty of impulsion but not too much speed, so that he can cope not only with the height of the rail, but also remain in balance and land safely after the drop **(fig. 64)**. You must keep your lower legs forward and your shoulders up so that you can help the

Fig. 64 A rail at the far edge of a bank requires straightness, balance and plenty of impulsion, but not too much speed

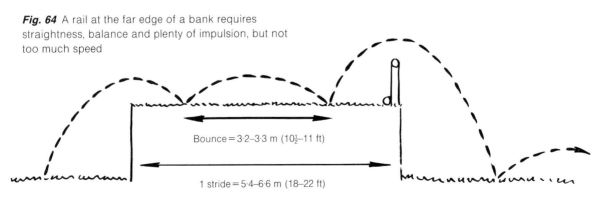

Bounce = 3·2–3·3 m (10½–11 ft)

1 stride = 5·4–6·6 m (18–22 ft)

horse to find his feet if he stumbles on landing. If you move up his neck over the rail, you are likely to be pulled off over the horse's head on the landing side.

If you approach the bank and rail too fast, the horse may catch the rail with his forearms because he is unable to make sufficient height, or he may jump the rail too freely, resulting in a fall because he is unable to balance himself on the landing side. Approaching the rail too slowly, cautiously or without enough impulsion may result in a refusal, or the horse making a vague attempt to jump the rail and then falling from the top of the rail to

42 The young horse jumping off a bank. He has lengthened his head and neck considerably and has jumped out a long way, a little too freely. The rider's position is good, although the lower legs could be a little further forward

the ground. Even if the horse does manage to jump the rail, he will probably land very steeply, causing considerable jarring and strain.

A bank will usually jump very well if you negotiate the first element correctly, and then sit up and keep your legs on to help guide the horse through the remaining elements. Banks are sometimes built

43 (*Top left*) On landing, the horse pays the penalty of over-jumping the bank by landing in a heap. The rider's position is fairly secure but the contact has become a little loose. If the horse tipped forward, the rider would have to pick up the contact very quickly in order to prevent a fall

44 (*Bottom left*) The experienced horse jumping on to a bank. The rider is behind the movement and is relying on the reins to stop herself from falling backward. This has probably happened because she has already jumped up a small step on to the first bank, and the horse has bounced on to the next bank before the rider could adjust her balance. The horse looks confident and appears to know what to do next

45 (*Below*) The horse has jumped economically off the bank, and the rider has leaned back and slipped the reins. This is the safest position for the inexperienced rider, but when confidence increases, the upper body will not need to be so far back as long as the lower legs are slightly forward of the vertical

side by side, requiring the horse to jump from one to another. Accuracy, balance and the correct amount of impulsion are required for this test, as there is not usually a guard rail to make the gap between the two banks obvious. If approached with the right ingredients, however, this will not cause a problem.

Related distances

Fences are at a related distance when they are close enough to each other to warrant a calculated number of strides being taken between them. The number of strides will be determined by the terrain, the type of going, the nature of the fence and its degree of difficulty.

Guidelines for calculating distances

As a general guide, the distances are decided in the following way. Each stride between each fence measures 3·6 metres (12 ft), and 1·8 metres (6 ft) are added for the take-off and landing over each fence. So, as a guide, for two fences with one non-jumping stride between them, the distance will be 7·2 metres (24 ft); two strides will be 10·9 metres (36 ft); four strides will be 18 metres (60 ft); and five strides will be 21·8 metres (72 feet).

These are basic distances, but they may be lengthened or shortened. When jumping on level ground, you should be ready to adjust the horse's stride on the approach so that he arrives at the first fence at the correct take-off point, lands, takes the correct number of even strides and then takes off over the next fence. If the distance is a little short, or the horse naturally makes up too much ground, you will need to prepare him on the approach by containing the canter, his outline and his speed. If the distance is quite long, or the horse finds it difficult to lengthen his stride and outline between fences, you will need to create a bigger, longer more powerful canter stride on the approach so that he is more able to make the distance between the fences.

Ascertaining the length of stride that is most suited to the distance between the fences should not be left to chance, but can be practised at home by building some fences at related distances. With practice, you will learn how the canter should feel for each particular distance. First of all, measure the distances using the method described above, and keep the height of the fences to 1 metre (3 ft). When you are confident that you can shorten or lengthen your horse's stride while keeping him in a good rhythm and balance, alter the distances a little so that you learn to shorten or lengthen the stride to a greater

or lesser degree. For example, from fence to fence, a short single stride would measure 5·4 metres (18 ft), and a long single stride would measure 8·4 metres (24 ft). The difference in the canter stride would need to be considerable if the horse were to cope with both of these distances with only one stride between the fences.

The ability to vary the length of the stride in this way is very important when riding across country, because of the differing distances and the effect that the terrain has on the length of the horse's stride. For instance, when a horse jumps a combination built on a downhill slope, the stride is naturally inclined to become longer, and you will feel as though there is a lot of weight coming forward on to the forehand and that the horse is leaning on the rein. At the take-off point, the horse will jump off his forehand, resulting in a poor-quality jump. This will be adequate if the fence is very straightforward and the distance between the fences of the combination is long, but if the distance is short or the fences are high or difficult, you must be able to shorten the horse's stride on the approach to compensate for the distance and the effect that the downhill slope has on his way of going. This means keeping the horse in balance with the weight off the forehand, controlling the approach, and keeping him responsive and soft in the hand.

To achieve this, you must sit up and keep your shoulders up, so that you can help to keep the horse from dropping on to the forehand. Keeping your lower legs slightly forward of the vertical will help you to balance not only yourself, but the horse as well. At the same time, you must encourage the horse to control his forward momentum by using his hindquarters underneath himself.

When fences are built at related distances on uphill terrain, the natural tendency is for the horse to slow down. In just the same way as, when driving a car uphill, you have to put your foot on the accelerator to keep the speed constant, so when you are approaching a related distance uphill where the distance has not been significantly shortened, you must create more impulsion in order to maintain the stride length. If you do not do this, and the horse finds the distance too long, he may refuse, fiddle another stride, put in half a stride, take off too far away from the second fence, or misjudge the second fence and fall. The impulsion created must then be contained so that the horse is able to jump the height of the fence and land far enough out over the other side. Use your legs to encourage him to activate his hindquarters, and, when he creates the impulsion, contain it between your hands and legs until it is needed so that you feel in control of the power.

Although slight downhill slopes encourage the strides to become longer, and slight uphill slopes encourage the strides to become shorter, steep inclines and declines encourage the horse to take considerably shorter strides, as this is his only way of remaining in balance. Once this is understood, it becomes more obvious as to why the horse requires a shortened stride and outline (i.e., a short, collected canter) when jumping into a coffin at which the slopes on either side of the ditch are considerable. Most combinations require the horse to approach with a short, balanced canter. If the horse approached such fences at a gallop, he would even-

tually fall, as the stride length, speed and balance would not be suitable for the fences he was expected to jump.

However, as the horse which gallops or canters across country usually covers more ground with each stride than the showjumper, it is only fair to expect to find some combinations on a course where the distances are a little longer than those set out in the guidelines on page 139. For instance, it would be perfectly feasible to have a one-strided combination of two ascending spreads on level ground with a distance between them of 8.1 metres (27 ft). As the horse's stride covers around 4·5 metres (15 ft) across country, it is perfectly possible for him to jump a combination such as this **(fig. 65)**. On the approach, you must prepare the horse by making sure that he is straight, balanced and concentrating on your demands, but, because the fence is not technical and does not require a short stride and outline, without dramatically reducing the length of the stride or the outline. This is an example of a straightforward combination, but as your horse becomes more experienced, he will be asked more complicated questions, and the quality of the approach will become more important as the terrain varies.

As a guide, the following types of fences require a shorter stride on the approach:

FENCES REQUIRING A SHORTER STRIDE ON THE APPROACH

- coffins (see page 102)
- steps up and down (see page 111)
- bounces (see page 43)
- water fences (see page 129)
- banks (see page 116)

Fig. 65 A one-strided combination of two ascending spreads on level ground

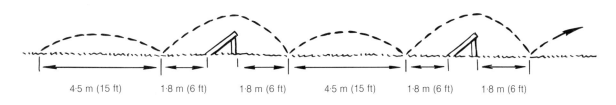

| 4·5 m (15 ft) | 1·8 m (6 ft) | 1·8 m (6 ft) | 4·5 m (15 ft) | 1·8 m (6 ft) | 1·8 m (6 ft) |

Having landed over the first element of any of the above, the stride is likely to be short, because the amount of effort required for jumping these fences often leaves the horse lacking energy and forward thrust. If another fence is to be jumped within a few strides, you must therefore bear in mind, when calculating the number of strides to be taken, that the canter steps will probably be a little shorter than the guideline length of 3·6 metres (12 ft).

When jumping combinations on level ground, where the fences are spreads and do not require such a high degree of accuracy or exact approach as the technical combinations, the distances you can expect to find may be longer distances than those given in the guidelines on page 121. Some people like to calculate the exact number of strides where a distance suggests taking seven or eight strides between the fences, but any number of strides over six can be altered by your ability to change the stride length between the two fences in question.

It is worth remembering that the shorter distances are normally used for the more demanding combinations, and the longer distances for the more onward-going combinations. If you have a horse that covers a lot of ground and quickly regains his rhythm even after the most demanding combination, he will cover more ground with each stride than a horse which finds it difficult to lengthen his stride or make up ground. As cross-country riding is about rhythm and strides of even length, it is up to you to know your horse's capability and what you can expect him to do without pushing him out of his rhythm, or, with the big-striding horse, how much you can expect him to shorten his stride. Once again, the importance of training and preliminary work becomes clear, as it is too late to teach the horse to adjust his stride by the time you get to the competition!

Angled Fences

Jumping fences on an angle, or where there is little margin for error, is a test of accuracy and of being able to ride a horse on a particular line and keep him channelled between your hands and legs so that he does not drift. You can teach your horse to jump accurately at home by jumping oil drums, gradually reducing the number until you are jumping a single drum. Alternatively, make some narrow, free-standing fences so that the horse has no wings to rely upon to keep him straight. These two methods will help to teach both you and the horse basic accuracy. More advanced methods are as follows.

- Set up a line of fences, starting with a normal-width fence and finishing with a narrow one of no more than 1 metre (3 ft) in width (**fig. 66**).
- Build a line of fences, offsetting each fence from the previous one. If you lose your line and rhythm, the horse will run out.
- Build a corner by resting two poles on an oil drum and gradually opening up the angle (see **figs. 28** and **29** on pages 51 and 52). Introduce a second fence in a direct line with the first, and then

GUIDE TO COMPETITION DISTANCES

Number of strides	Minimum distances	Maximum distances
One stride	5·4 m (18 ft)	8·5 m (28 ft)
Two strides	9.0 m (30 ft)	11·8 m (39 ft)
Three strides	13·6 m (45 ft)	15·8 m (52 ft)
Four strides	16·4 m (54 ft)	19.4 m (64 ft)
Five strides	20·9 m (69 ft)	23·6 m (78 ft)
Six strides	24·5 m (81 ft)	27·6 m (91 ft)

gradually offset it from the first fence. A more experienced horse can have a corner as the second fence as well, which can be offset from the first corner. The distance between the two corners, which is where the horse should jump the fences, should be 7·2 metres (24 ft).

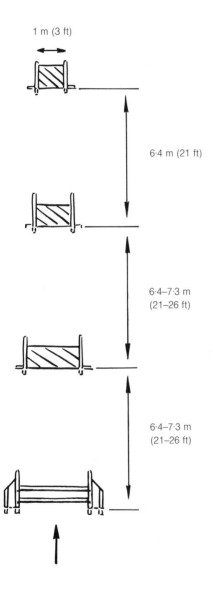

1 m (3 ft)

6·4 m (21 ft)

6·4–7·3 m (21–26 ft)

6·4–7·3 m (21–26 ft)

Fig. 66 A row of progressively narrower fences without wings is useful for teaching accuracy

- For advanced training, build three to four fences, slightly offset or on a curve, so that you have to find the correct line through the fence on the approach. If you leave this until the last few strides before take-off, the horse may be unsure where you want him to go, and, if he sees the daylight out to the side of the fence, he may take that route as the easy option.
- For very experienced horses, constructing fences over dry or water ditches creates a two-fold problem. The horse has to remain on the line, but he also has to be brave enough to jump with accuracy and boldness, regardless of the ditch underneath **(fig. 67)**.

Angled fences require the most advanced skills from the cross-country rider. During the course walk, you must determine the best approach, and then walk the line a few times to make absolutely certain that the line is suitable. It should be possible to look back at the fence as you are walking through it, to check that you are still on the same line and that you have not drifted one way or the other. On the final time of looking at the fence, there must be no doubt in your mind, and it should be possible to walk the exact line to the fence from landing over the previous one, and then to remain on the line throughout the fence.

You must also be able to picture the line through the fence in your mind as you ride the approach, when balance, straightness, rhythm, impulsion and concentration are of paramount importance. Get on your line as early as possible, and then ride positively all the way to the fence with plenty of impulsion and the horse in good rhythm. If there is a ditch beneath the fence, there is no reason why the horse should know it is there if the approach is correct, and so this should not cause significant problems.

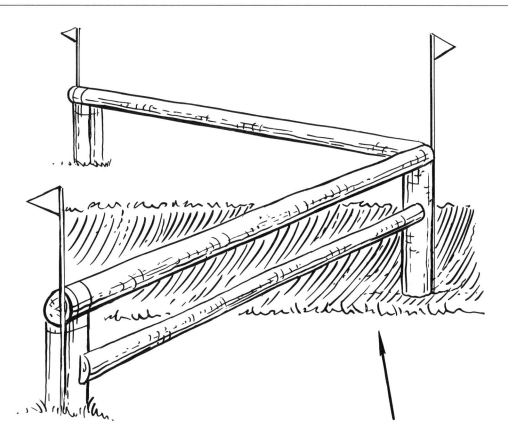

Fig. 67 A fence over a dry or water ditch is a difficult fence, requiring accuracy on the approach and a bold jump over the ditch

Corners

The introduction of corners has already been discussed, but below are some pointers as to what to look for when you are faced with this type of fence.

The width of the corner will determine how much leeway you have at the point you choose to jump, and whether the corner has a wing on it will determine how close to the apex you can jump without risking a run-out. Try to approach a left-handed corner on a very slight line from left to right, and a right-handed corner very slightly from right to left, so that you show the horse the fence and not the way out to the side. Pick a line where the

ground does not pull you past the corner or draw you too far from the apex, making it potentially too wide to jump **(fig. 68)**. Make sure that the landing is not obscured in any way, so that the horse will feel confident about where he is going to land.

Angled combination fences

Where there is more than one angled fence to jump within a stride or two of the previous one, you must pre-determine the line that is most suited to you and your horse. This is because it is important to ride the correct line on the approach to the first fence, as there will be too little room to make any alterations once you have jumped this part. Keeping the horse straight or on a line through an angled combination may require one or more fences to be jumped on the angle.

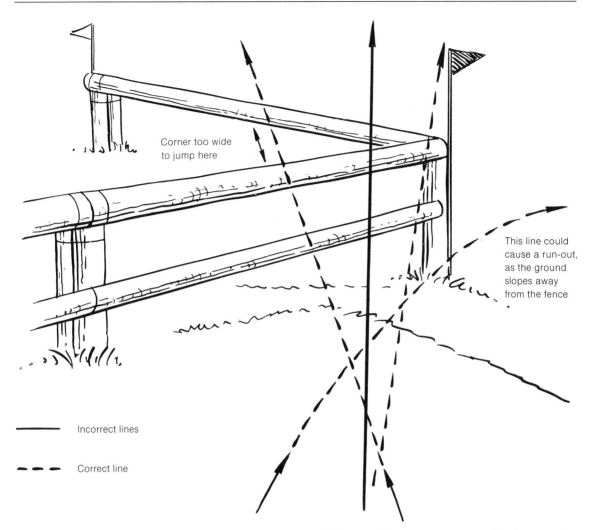

Corner too wide to jump here

This line could cause a run-out, as the ground slopes away from the fence

——————— Incorrect lines

– – – Correct line

Fig. 68 The line taken at a corner fence is very important, as the horse has to jump near the apex, where the angle is narrow, making a run-out a possibility

Bear in mind the following points.

- If a horse is a little untidy over an upright fence on the angle, he may get away with it, but if he is untidy over a parallel, he will have more chance of getting into trouble because he has the spread to clear as well as the height.
- Always try to find a line where you keep showing the horse to the fence and not the daylight to the side, so that he learns to go to the fence and not towards the way out.

- Where there are several alternative routes at a combination, always choose a route that is suitable for your horse's experience, gives the correct distance for your horse between each element, and gives you every chance of jumping through without incurring penalties.

All too often, riders attempt a very difficult route without really planning their approach and the line very thoroughly, so they incur penalties for refusing, running out or falling. It is much more beneficial to both your and the horse's confidence if a slightly easier alternative is jumped without incurring penalties except for loss of time (see **fig. 76** on page 153).

Angled fences over ditches

There is very little choice as to where this type of fence can be jumped, because the ditch and fence only meet in one place. Study the fence, and look for the best take-off point where the ground is good and hopefully slightly raised rather than falling away, which may encourage the horse to run past the fence. The distance from take-off to landing should be the minimum possible, and you should check that the ground on the landing side is good and firm. Ideally, the rail or fence will largely cover the ditch, and the horse's eye will not be drawn into it. The horse must be able to see what he is being asked to jump, so if you approach the rail at too acute an angle, he will either run down the rail, or will run past the fence altogether. If the rail over the ditch is a parallel or a footbridge it is unwise to try to jump it on an angle, as, if the horse makes an untidy jump, he is likely to hit one or other of the parallel rails and may fall. You should therefore try to find a line where the ditch is on an angle and not too wide, and where the take-off and landing are good.

Once you have decided on a suitable take-off and landing, walk back to a point at which the line can be picked up well in advance, and then walk the line to the fence. It is also advisable to walk round to the proposed landing spot, to check that the approach, take-off and landing are in a line not only from the take-off side, but from the landing side as well (fig. 69).

Arrowheads

Over the last few years, this type of fence has become very popular. The most com-

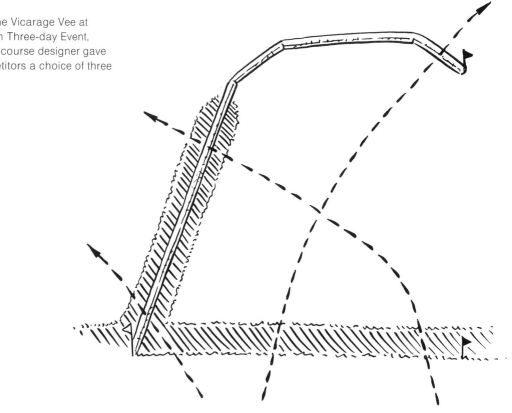

Fig. 69 The Vicarage Vee at Badminton Three-day Event, where the course designer gave the competitors a choice of three routes

monly used type of arrowhead is in the form of a triple bar **(fig. 70)**. On its own, this fence is only a test of accuracy, but it becomes more of a test if placed one or two strides after jumping on to or off a bank. In this case, the bank must be negotiated successfully, and the horse has to land after the bank at the correct position to enable him to put in the appropriate number of strides before taking off over the arrowhead. If he stands off the triple bar, he may struggle to reach the back rail, but if you do not keep him in control and in balance when he jumps off the bank (i.e., if he over-jumps the bank), he will be out of balance for the arrowhead.

The horse must be kept straight and balanced for the duration of the test, or he may run past the arrowhead. If he tries to jump it on an angle because he is crooked,

he will run the risk of hitting the fence and falling. Do not sit back too far and let the reins go to the buckle, or you will be unable to steer the horse to the arrowhead. Keeping your lower legs forward will help you to stay in balance, and from there you will be able to steer the horse. Although he must be allowed to use his head and neck, you should brace your upper body to help the horse to land in balance.

If you are worried about the arrowhead for any reason, it would be sensible to jump one of the arms. Although slower, this is usually safer, as long as there is enough room for the approach. Make sure when jumping an arm that the line of approach gives the horse a clear view on the landing side. In other words, do not choose a line where the rail of the other

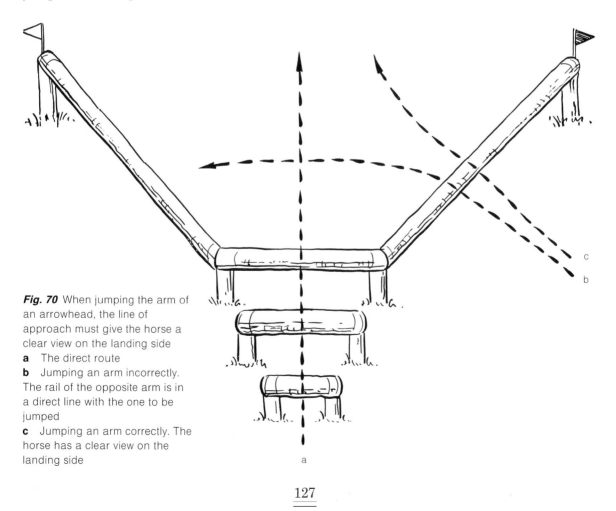

Fig. 70 When jumping the arm of an arrowhead, the line of approach must give the horse a clear view on the landing side
a The direct route
b Jumping an arm incorrectly. The rail of the opposite arm is in a direct line with the one to be jumped
c Jumping an arm correctly. The horse has a clear view on the landing side

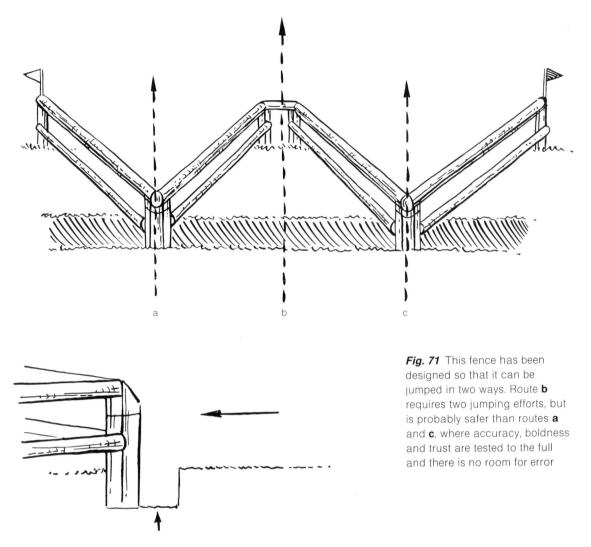

a   b   c

Fig. 71 This fence has been designed so that it can be jumped in two ways. Route **b** requires two jumping efforts, but is probably safer than routes **a** and **c**, where accuracy, boldness and trust are tested to the full and there is no room for error

The dry ditch in front of the point at routes a and c

wing is in a direct line with the one that you intend to jump. Lastly, remember that arrowheads are mostly a test of accuracy, so practice in jumping narrow fences at home will be good preparation.

Points

As with arrowheads, points have become very popular in the last few years. Points are usually narrower than arrowheads and are designed in a more upright way,

requiring greater accuracy. These fences are normally constructed of two posts with a wing or arm on either side.

A dry or water ditch can be added to this type of fence on the take-off side. This fence can be jumped in two ways, depending on the construction: by jumping the ditch separately and then negotiating one of the wings or arms; or by jumping the point with the ditch on the take-off side in one effort **(fig. 71)**. The former method is usually much safer if it can be jumped in this way, but will probably take a little more time as it requires two jumping efforts instead of one. The latter requires great accuracy and boldness, as the take-off position is critical and allows no margin for error at all. This means that, if the horse veers one way or the other, he can be in serious trouble. If he hesitates on take-off, there is also the likelihood that he may slip into the ditch or hit the point and roll back into the ditch. If a horse hits a rail or a brush fence, there is a good chance that he will roll over it, but the same unfortunately does not apply to a point.

Water fences

There are many types of water fence, and many ways in which water is introduced on a course. Some fences are natural hazards, and others are purpose-built for horses to jump.

Brooks and rivers

A brook or river is sometimes included in a course. It is important to check that:

- the banks are firm and not likely to collapse or give way
- the ground on the approach is not poached, waterlogged or rutted
- there are no sharp flints, stones, broken bottles or glass on the ground or the riverbed
- the water is no deeper than 30 centimetres (1 ft)
- the bottom is firm and level, and free from holes or deep areas

Fences are not often constructed on the banks or in the middle of brooks and rivers because it is difficult to determine the level of the water on the day of the competition, so they are only really suitable for crossing as a natural hazard.

Man-made water fences

When you walk the course, you must check the depth of the water and the surface on which the horse will land, by simply putting on a pair of wellington boots or waders and having a walk about. It is not acceptable to throw in a stick for your dog to test the depth! Check the water for depth and evenness of depth, and note the smoothness of the surface beneath the water and any holes or irregularities.

Water slows the horse down and encourages his stride to become longer and flatter. The deeper and wider the water, the more spray he will produce, and in extreme cases, a wave-type situation can be instigated. It is vital to introduce the horse to water at an early stage (see below) so that he becomes familiar and confident with it.

The approach to water must be at a controlled pace, or the horse will enter the water too fast and the drag on his legs may tip him over. In addition, a great deal of spray may be thrown up which will interfere with the horse's concentration, soaking him and you so that judging the exit fence becomes very difficult. Shallow water with no jump in or out can be approached in a collected canter or an ongoing trot. As the horse may become unbalanced and therefore slightly uncoordinated on entering the water, it is up to you to be aware that he may need support and correct riding to help him to regain his balance and momentum.

Jumping fences into water

Brush fences or logs are ideal fences for introducing novice horses to jumping into water. Start with a fence two to three strides from the water, and, when the horse becomes confident, introduce a small fence at the water's edge. Keep the entry fence simple until the horse is very confident, because if he is over-faced at this stage, he will never jump the more complex fences into water which will come when he is more experienced. The water should always be kept to a depth of 30 centimetres (12 ins), and the approach fence should be no more than 1 metre (3 ft) high or wide. The fence should encourage the horse to jump it, so a true parallel or upright should be avoided, whereas an ascending solid spread no more than 1 metre (3 ft) wide is ideal.

Although the approach must not be too fast, the pace must contain enough energy so that, if the horse backs off a little, he will still have enough impulsion to jump. If it is possible to keep the horse in a collected, forward-thinking canter, then that is the right sort of approach to have, but if the horse has not yet reached that stage in his training, approach in a forward-thinking, balanced trot.

Often there is a drop into water, and you must alter your position accordingly (46). This means sitting back, slipping the reins

46 This rider has kept her weight and upper body back to allow for the drop into the water

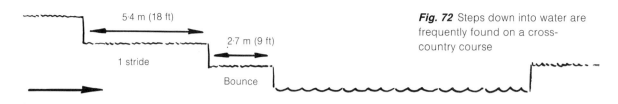

Fig. 72 Steps down into water are frequently found on a cross-country course

if necessary and keeping the lower legs forward. Having jumped into the water, the horse must be given a second or two to find his balance before the approach to the next or exit fence begins. There may be a fence to jump in the water, and if the horse breaks into a trot, stay in trot and try to keep the impulsion rather than attempting to canter and losing the balance and momentum. Keep the horse straight,

balanced and going forward, and do not tip forward and predict the take-off point – leave that to the horse. Horses sometimes jump fences into water very big, so it is important to keep your balance and to keep your shoulders up on take-off so that you do to not get pulled forward and out of position.

If steps are used as a way of entering the water, keep them small with a distance of 2·7 metres (9 ft) for a bounce of 5·4 metres (18 ft) for one stride **(fig. 72)**. At first, the horse may jump from the last step on all four legs into the water, which will create a big splash. With experience, he will learn to drop into the water, creating much less spray **(47–54)**.

47 These steps are suitable for a young horse, as they are not too steep and there is plenty of room between them. The horse has come down the first step and is concentrating on the second. The rider's lower legs are in a forward position, ready to encourage him forward

48 The second step is successfully negotiated, with the horse in good balance. The rider has felt her starting to drift to the left, and has opened the right rein to keep her straight

49 The horse is straighter now, so there is no more need for an open rein. The horse and rider are concentrating on where they are going, and the horse is not perturbed by the puddle on the third step

50 A good deal of spray is thrown up, but the horse is concentrating on the next element. The rider is sitting up as still as possible so as not to interfere with the balance

51 The horse makes a positive jump out of the water but lands a little flat on the first step, probably due to lack of experience and impulsion. The rider has got slightly behind the movement and she is sitting a little heavily, which may hinder the horse as she brings her hindlegs out of the water

52 By the time the horse bounces up the next step, impulsion has been regained and the rider's seat has come a little more forward. The horse now looks in a very good position from which to jump the next step

53 The horse makes a real effort to bounce up the final step. The take-off was a little too far away, and she has stretched her head and neck to help her to make the distance. The rider is light in her seat and the lower legs are in a good position to create impulsion

54 The horse lands in good balance, and the hindlegs will soon come forward so that she can get back into her stride. Throughout the sequence, the rider has kept very still so that the horse could concentrate on her first multi-part combination, which she jumped in a very grown-up, calculated way

Jumping fences out of water

If the fence out of water is a log or a brush, the same principle applies to jumping a fence in the water. Ideally, the horse does not want to stand off, as he may have to reach to make the fence and may then struggle to get all his legs over to the other side of the fence, leaving him out of balance and with no forward momentum.

A very popular exit out of water is a step followed by a palisade-type fence on level ground, at a distance from 2·7 metres (9 ft) for a bounce to 5·4 to 6 metres (18 to 20 ft) for one stride and 10·5 to 11·5 metres (33 to 36 ft) for two strides **(fig. 73)**. As the drag of the water reduces the horse's spring when jumping out of it, the impulsion must be maintained through the water. Try to jump the step out of the water accurately, as taking off from too far away will leave the horse too much ground to cover before the next fence because he will have lost much of his forward impulsion. Taking off too close may result in the horse tripping up the step and falling, or, at best, landing in an unbalanced way with no impulsion at all. Do not go too fast, or lose your way and ride into deep water, or otherwise the drag will unbalance the horse and the spray will interfere with his line of vision.

POINTS TO REMEMBER

When teaching young horses to jump water, avoid fences where:

- water leaks to the take-off side, as the horse will find it difficult to judge the take-off
- the take-off is downhill, as this may encourage the horse to slide into the bottom of the fence, which could frighten him
- there are two fences with one or two strides between them, as this is a lot to ask of a horse that is only just getting used to water
- the distances are too long and the horse is unsure of the number of strides to be taken. As the horse is likely to back off a little, the distances should be adjusted accordingly: 6·3 to 7·2 metres (21 to 24 ft) for one stride and 9·6 to 10·6 metres (32 to 35 ft) for two strides when the second fence is at the water's edge
- there is only enough room for a bounce between fences – this is too difficult at an early stage

Try to stay in balance throughout, and sit up and maintain the forward impulsion by using your seat and legs.

Water fences for advanced horses

As the horse gains in experience, more demanding obstacles can be built to test his ability. The severity of the water jump can be changed in two ways: by making the entry and exit fences more demanding;

Fig. 73 A step up from water followed by a palisade fence on level ground requires accuracy and impulsion

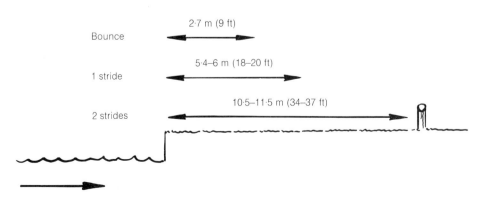

	2·7 m (9 ft)
Bounce	⟷
1 stride	5·4–6 m (18–20 ft)
2 strides	10·5–11·5 m (34–37 ft)

and by having a greater depth of water. The water in which the horse lands should not be more than 0.5 metre (20 ins), although the depth may increase dramatically if you lose control and start to go off course. It is, however, an unfair test deliberately to increase the difficulty of the water fence by significantly increasing the depth on the line the horse will take through the water. It is a much fairer test to increase the severity of the entrance and exit fences in one of the following ways.

- The ground can be made to slope away during the last two strides on the approach.
- The height and width of the fence can be increased so that the jump into and out of water becomes more demanding.
- There can be a combination in the form of posts and rails (painted white, white and red, grey or left natural), palisades, brush or birch fences, stone walls or logs; they can be set at a distance for the horse either to bounce or to take one or two strides. A step is often used as the exit fence from the water, and as a follow-on, any combination of the above can be incorporated. The fences can also be wide or very narrow in the form of arrowheads (see page 126), in which case a test of accuracy is also included. When a water fence is of this severity, an easier – albeit slower – alternative should be offered.

Choosing your route through a water complex

First of all, study the fence as a whole, look at all the alternatives and the distances, and ascertain the depth of the water. Determine the most suitable route for your horse, bearing in mind that, if you think your horse may back off on the approach and the entry fence is a combi-nation, a shorter distance would be best. If, on the other hand, your horse is likely to make up a lot of ground between the fences, a longer distance will be more suitable for him. Water fences should never be constructed with less than 5·4 metres (18 ft) between them, or the horse may think that he has to jump in and bounce out.

If the fences are built at an equal distance from each other, determine the best take-off point by locating the best ground. Often the fence will be built in such a way that it lends itself to being jumped in a certain place, and, as long as the distances are suitable, this is the place to jump it. Having determined your route through the entry fence, determine the best exit route by equipping yourself with some wellingtons and walking the exit route from the landing side of the entry fence. Having sorted out your proposed route, walk back and find a line from a long way away.

It is also advisable to walk all the alternative routes, so that you can change the original route if necessary. If, for instance, your horse is not going as well as you had hoped, and you feel that he is slightly lacking in confidence on the earlier part of the course, an easier route through the water should be taken. It is also possible that, having landed in the water, you cannot take your exit route originally planned, either because you have landed too far off line for the exit fence, or because you feel that you cannot get the horse organized in time. If you think fast enough in these situations, however, it is often possible to jump an alternative, easier route without incurring penalties.

Some people are emphatic about the number of strides to take through the water, but because of the funny effect it has on horses, it can be very difficult to put the theory into practice. It is much more important to think of keeping the horse balanced, straight and with forward momentum, to guard against him becoming long and strung out as you go through the water; the further the horse goes through the water, the more difficult it is to keep an energetic canter. If the stretch of water is very long, keep the balance for two-thirds of the way and, in the final third, 'lift' the horse so that you have the maximum amount of contained energy and concentration for the exit fence. This will help the stride to come to you so that the correct take-off point becomes obvious, providing that you have ridden the horse correctly and have not lost balance yourself. Where the exit from the water is up a slope and the exit fence is sited two to three strides later on dry ground, concentrate on the exit fence and the horse will just come out of the water within the rhythm of the canter.

Multiple water combinations

Sometimes on a course there is a multi-part water complex. This will have various options and alternatives, but usually requires more than one entry and exit into and out of the water. You should approach these types of fences with the same attitude as for other water fences, and break the fence down into sections so that it is easier to work out the best route for your horse. Walk all the alternatives and distances, and then see how many alternative routes you have to choose from.

When you ride through this type of combination, the further you get through it, the more difficult it is to keep the impulsion within the canter. If the impulsion fades, there is a strong possibility that the horse will reach one element and refuse, as he will not have the energy to jump it. On the approach, think of maintaining the impulsion and the rhythm of the canter, and never under-estimate the drag or pull of the water or the amount of spray, which can affect the horse's ability to jump the fences.

Natural hazards

Cross-country riding is about getting from A to B by negotiating natural hazards which may include boulders, drainage ditches and tree stumps. The crossing of these has to be done in the most economical way so that the rhythm of the canter or gallop is not broken.

Riding through wooded areas

A course often winds its way through a wood, where there may be a number of protruding tree stumps. In some cases these will be painted white, so make a note of these when walking the course. It is virtually impossible to remember the position of each tree stump, especially at the speed you will be going in competition, so the best plan of attack for avoiding these is to:

- take note of the most prominent ones
- try to plan the most direct route through them so as not to waste any time
- reduce the speed of the pace if the track in the wood is twisty, so that it is possible to keep the horse in balance and rhythmical through the wood
- avoid 'throwing' the horse round the corners, as there is a danger that he may slip and lose his feet
- give yourself as much preparation time on the approach as possible when there is a fence sited off a corner
- use tree stumps as turning markers where necessary

See page 140 for advice on coping with the changing light in wooded areas.

A GUIDE TO DISTANCES IN COMBINATION FENCES

Below is a list of the distances you can expect to find when competing at Novice to Advanced level. The distances are total lengths, and they include take-off and landing.

Upright to upright
Bounce 4–4·5 m (13 ft 6 ins–15 ft)
One stride 7·3–8·2 m (24–27 ft)
Two strides 10·5–11·5 m (35–36 ft)

Upright to parallel or parallel to upright
Bounce 3·6–4·2 m (12–14 ft)
One stride 7·3–7·9 m (24–26 ft)
Two strides 10·5–11·5 m (33–36 ft)

Parallel to parallel
Bounce not recommended
One stride 7·3–7·5 m (24–26 ft)
Two strides 10·5–10·9 m (35–36 ft)

Step up and down
Bounce 2·7 m (9 ft)
One stride 5·4 m (18 ft)

Bank with rail off
Bounce 3·2–3·3 m (10 ft 6 ins–11 ft)
One stride 5·4–6·6 m (18–21 ft)

Bank with jump on and off
Bounce 3·6–3·9 m (12–13 ft)
One stride 6·4–7·2 m (21–24 ft)

Rails to step up
Bounce 3·6–3·9 m (12–13 ft)
One stride 7–7·2 m (23–24 ft)

Rails to step down
Bounce 3–3·3 m (10–11 ft)
One stride 6–6·4 m (20–21 ft)

Step up to rails
Bounce 2·7 m (9 ft)
One stride 5·4–6 m (18–20 ft)

Step down to rail
Bounce 3·6 m (12 ft)
One stride 6·4 m (21 ft)

Coffins
One stride on easy slopes 5·4–6m (18–20 ft)
One stride on more difficult slopes 4·5 m (15 ft)

Ditch and rails
Bounce 3·6 m (12 ft)
One stride 5·4–6 m (18–20 ft)

Ditches

In some cases, drainage ditches are a natural feature of the land. They are often difficult to see as they are level with the ground, and many of them are also very narrow. The best way of coping with them is to approach with the horse in balance and going in a controlled manner, so that he has a chance to see them and not jump at too acute an angle. This is important because otherwise he could misjudge the ditch and catch the edge with one or more of his legs.

Natural banks

These appear as an undulation on the ground and may be the result of a fence line which has been removed. Although they are not very steep, these banks are severe enough to break the rhythm of the stride. Approach in a balanced, controlled canter and give the horse time to find his way over them.

Ridge and furrow

Ridge and furrow are the remains of a farming method whereby each field was divided into large strips which were distributed to the villagers for cultivation. If a cross-country course dictates that these hillocks and hollows have to be crossed, caution is the main priority, because no matter how you hope to cross them, every other stride leaves the horse's front legs thudding into the hollows. It is not advisable to gallop without caution across this type of ground, as the horse much prefers to be in balance and within a rhythm, which will be virtually impossible if you are thinking of the clock.

Ridge and furrow are awkward to ride whatever you do, but it is important to consider the possibility of jarring the horse and his legs, so always keep the horse at a sensible speed, at which he is able to cross the ridge and furrow without having to break the rhythm every time he meets one awkwardly.

Differing weather and light conditions

As well as the fences and natural hazards, the weather conditions can influence the way a course rides, so it is important to consider these.

Sunlight

The reflection of the sun on a fence can give it a glaring appearance, but a horse can usually adapt as long as you give him a chance to adjust his vision. This need only take a split second, and all it entails is you sitting in balance and not bustling the horse out of balance in his attempt to jump the fence.

Jumping into and out of woods

When considering the approach to a fence in a wood, or from light into dark, look for a line where the landing is obvious to the horse. Approach with plenty of impulsion and with the horse going foward into your hand. Be sure to ride an accurate approach, because if the horse is a little unsure of jumping into the wood he may wobble about, and, if he is not between your legs and hands at the start and is making his own way to the fence, he will be able to run straight past it. If the horse backs off on the last few strides prior to taking off, use your legs and drive him forward. Do not tip forward as he will simply slow down, the weight will drop on to his forehand and he will grind to a stop.

Jumping back out of the wood rarely causes problems, as the horse seems confident to jump back into the daylight. If the fence is quite sizeable, however, you must keep your shoulders up and drive the horse forward so that he does not back off and then 'climb' over the fence.

Rain

Initially, rain makes the ground slippery, then muddy and, in extreme cases, holding. The horse loses his grip in wet ground, so you must be adept at making sure that he does not lose his footing and his balance. Every turn needs to be taken more carefully, and quick, jerky actions must be avoided.

Once the rain gets into the ground and the surface gets turned over, the horse will often find more grip. When the going becomes holding, he will find it more difficult to find enough spring from the ground for jumping, because the ground is holding him rather than giving him lift. This is especially true of soil with a high clay content, which gets very sticky and literally clings to the horse's feet and legs when it becomes holding. Sandy soil drains much more easily, and the particles do not stick together and therefore do not cling to the horse's feet and legs. When conditions become very difficult and the ground becomes very holding, the horse must be ridden with more impulsion so that he is able to make the extra effort needed to cope with the ground.

The most difficult type of rain is when there is a good covering of long grass on ground that has not seen rain for a long time. Then, when the heavens open, the horse cannot get any grip at all as the grass becomes very slippery. Unless the course is very straightforward, it is inadvisable to compete in these conditions, particularly if you are inexperienced and are trying to increase your own and your horse's confidence. Studs in the horse's shoes are very helpful when conditions are like this. Small round studs should be used in front, while larger studs with a small point are ideal for the hind feet (55). If you are in doubt about which studs to use, seek the advice of an experienced rider.

55 A stud correctly fitted on the outer edge of a hind shoe

If you do choose to run your horse in these conditions, some of the more direct routes may be inadvisable. This is because they may require extreme accuracy and boldness, and the state of the ground is not going to allow you to ride in such a precise way. You must therefore make sure that you are clear in your own mind about the alternative routes.

There is a lot to be said for replacing your cross-country jersey with a lightweight waterproof coat. It is particularly important to stay dry and warm if you have more than one horse to ride.

Although it is easy to cope with being wet when the adrenalin is flowing, you may regret it when you develop a heavy cold a few days later! It is also important to keep your horse warm and dry after he has finished competing, so remember to take plenty of rugs and towels.

Hard, firm going

As the event season runs through the summer months, it is very difficult to avoid running horses on hard ground. The greatest problems with this type of going are concussion, stress and jarring, and if your horse is affected in any of these ways he may refuse to jump at all. Sore shins, puffy joints, bursal enlargements, heat in the legs and feet, reduced action, inclination to refuse or poor jumping are all signs that the horse is affected by the hard ground.

If you wish to compete when the ground is hard, you must take certain steps to ensure that your horse does not suffer. Common sense is a vital ingredient when dealing with horses, so before and during the event season, always do plenty of roadwork and slow canter work before hand. Detect any early sights of trouble by checking your horse's legs and feet for signs of heat, pain and swelling at least twice a day. After each work-out, hose all four legs for five minutes each, and then apply a cooling lotion or poultice that is compatible with your horse's skin. Packing cold poultice into the soles of the feet also helps to bring out any heat.

Do not run your horse every weekend, but pick the most important competitions and replace some of the fitness work in between by working on an all-weather surface or by seeking the advice of a person experienced in the use of treadmills and swimming pools as a means of keeping or getting horses fit. Make sure that the farrier comes regularly, and that your horse's feet are correctly trimmed,

balanced and shod so that there is no excess strain being placed on the feet or the joints of the lower legs. Some of the pads that are available can help to absorb shock, but you should seek the farrier's advice as these can dramatically alter the balance of the feet.

When riding, do not gallop flat out at any time, but always ride your horse in a balanced, controlled way. Do not ask your horse to stand off a long way from his fences when the ground is hard, especially if there is a drop on the landing side. Try to ride him to his fences so that he jumps them in the most economical way possible, as the higher he jumps, the further it will be to the ground on the landing side. The steeper the landing, the greater the jarring effect on the horse will be. Hard ground is also often slippery, especially if there is very little grass cover. The use of studs can help the horse to gain some grip, particularly on the turns. These should be kept small, and are usually better equipped to cope with the baked earth if they have a rounded or pointed end.

Hail

Hail has a habit of appearing at very inopportune moments. Apart from the obvious problem caused to the ground if it continues for any length of time, horses still manage to jump in hail, so do not be unduly worried if a storm comes as you are starting your round. However, it is hard to believe that a horse can concentrate just as well when there is hail blowing into his face, and the ground is also likely to become slippery, so take extra care and consider jumping some of the slower alternatives if conditions deteriorate.

Snow

If there is a quick snowstorm, it may make vision difficult and the ground a little slippery. Snow which has settled for any length of time balls up in the horse's feet, making jumping virtually impossible. If you are exercising in snow, pack the soles of your horse's feet with engine oil or petroleum jelly which will help them remain free from the snow.

Wind

Wind in itself is fairly harmless, as it does not adversely affect the state of the going, but it is very difficult to ride into a strong wind. Problems also arise when the wind starts moving objects – it is practically impossible to show-jump in strong winds, for instance, as the wings and fillers of the jumps get blown down. It is vital that every item likely to be caught by the wind is secured either to the ground or to something substantial. Horses become anxious when banners, roping and flags start flapping about. If there is a danger of something blowing in your path as you approach a fence, pull up rather than frightening the horse at the fence.

SUMMARY

- A number of factors must be taken into consideration when tackling a cross-country course: the fences to be jumped; the type of terrain; the going and the weather conditions; the speed at which you intend to go; and whether you are competing for experience or whether you hope to win.
- The presence of a ground line makes a fence look more inviting, but be careful if the top rail is prominent or the fence leans to the take-off side, as a false ground line may be created, causing the horse to take off too close.
- Upright fences demand a balanced approach and an accurate take-off. At the same time, beware of over-cautiousness, which may cause the horse to back off the fence and put in a stop.
- A fence with a downhill landing is a test of boldness and athleticism. If the horse over-jumps and fails to land in balance, you can save him from falling if you keep your upper body behind the movement and your legs forward. This will allow you to give the horse the freedom of his head and neck, yet you will be ready to support his forehand if necessary by holding on to the reins and keeping your weight back.
- An uphill fence requires increased impulsion as the horse climbs the hill. He may land with little forward movement, so you must anticipate this by using stronger aids on landing to maintain the energy.
- Spreading fences are fairly straightforward to jump, but there must be energy within the pace, as the horse has to clear both height and spread. A large spread with a drop on landing requires a collected pace so that the horse does not lose his balance on the landing side.
- Approach a ditch fence with determination and plenty of impulsion, as, once a horse has stopped at a large ditch and looked into it, it may be virtually impossible to persuade him to jump it at all.
- At a fence consisting of several elements, such as a coffin, adequate speed must be maintained on the approach in order to carry the horse through all four elements. The key is a strong lower-leg position so that you can drive the horse forward by activating his hindquarters if the canter begins to fade. Sitting up and keeping your shoulders back will ensure that there is no danger of being pitched forward if the horse hits the first rail.
- Demanding fences such as angled combination fences and arrowheads must be introduced to the horse before he encounters them in competition, so that he knows what is expected of him.
- The weather conditions on the day must be taken into account, as they can make a great difference to the way you ride the course.

Part 3
COMPETING

6

TRAVELLING

The transport

Before travelling to an event, your lorry or trailer must be checked for safety reasons. The lorry needs to be insured, taxed and plated, and you may need a special licence to drive it if its maximum authorized mass exceeds 3·5 tonnes. It is a good idea to be a member of a vehicle-recovery organization so that, if you are unlucky enough to break down, you know that help is available. A portable telephone is very useful, and, although it is probably regarded as a luxury item and an unnecessary expense, it uses outweigh its cost. If you have a telephone, check that the battery is fully charged and, if you have a re-charging lead which plugs into the cigarette lighter, make sure that the voltage is compatible for both.

Remember to take a method of payment for petrol or diesel, and never let the tank get lower than a quarter full. Some fuel gauges are unreliable, and if you let the tank empty the fuel pipes have to be bled to remove the air before the engine will turn over again. It is always sensible to have the height, width and length of your lorry written in the cab, along with the unladen weight, so that you do not get stuck under a bridge on a weight-restricted road.

Check the oil, water and tyre pressures and make sure that you have a spare tyre which is roadworthy. If you use a trailer, check that the hitch is in good order and that there is a safety chain from the trailer to the towing vehicle in case the hitch should break. Check that the lights, indicators and number plates are in order and take a look around the trailer to check that all is as it should be. When attaching the towing vehicle, adjust the wing mirrors so that you can see down the sides of the trailer for overtaking purposes. The weight of the towing vehicle should exceed the laden weight of the trailer.

Keep an up-to-date road map in the lorry or towing vehicle and plan your route before you set out, making sure that you have the full address of your destination in case you get lost and have to ask the way. Estimate on covering 50 to 60 km (30 to 40 miles) per hour, unless the route is all motorway, in which case you may cover up to 80 km (50 miles) per hour.

If you are using hired transport, always choose a reputable organization which has been recommended by word of mouth. Their equipment will be safer, better serviced and more reliable, and their staff will be experienced with the handling and transporting of horses. Always check that the lorry has been disinfected before loading your horse, or he may pick up germs from the previous occupants. Never use the transport if this has not been done.

Equipment

Your horse should travel in either travelling bandages with knee and hock boots, or, if you prefer, leg protectors which cover the coronary band, the knees and the hocks. The headcollar (halter) can have a poll guard attached if you are worried about your horse banging his head either on entry or when installed in the trailer or lorry. If your horse is likely to chew through the headcollar (halter) rope, it can be replaced with a rubber-covered chain **(fig. 74)**. Attach a piece of string to the ring on the headcollar so that, if the horse pulls back, the string and not the headcollar will break. When a number of horses are travelling together without headboards, tie them up on both sides of their headcollars so that they cannot bite their neighbours.

Put an anti-sweat or cooler rug on the horse and, depending on the weather, add one or two rugs to keep him warm. It is important for the horse to have a free flow of air when travelling, but cold air may chill him. Most horses become a little hot when travelling and may sweat, so it is important to rug them accordingly to prevent them from getting a chill. A rug can be folded off the shoulders and secured with the use of a roller so that the horse's back is kept warm without over-heating the rest of him. Attach a filet string to each rug to stop it blowing up in the wind. The horse's tail should be bandaged with a

Fig. 74 Equipment for travelling

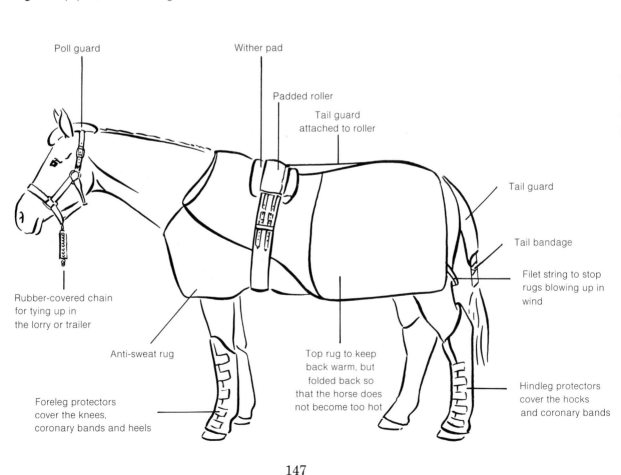

Poll guard

Wither pad

Padded roller

Tail guard attached to roller

Tail guard

Tail bandage

Filet string to stop rugs blowing up in wind

Rubber-covered chain for tying up in the lorry or trailer

Anti-sweat rug

Top rug to keep back warm, but folded back so that the horse does not become too hot

Foreleg protectors cover the knees, coronary bands and heels

Hindleg protectors cover the hocks and coronary bands

guard put on the top if there is any possibility of it being rubbed **(56)**. A stocking can be put on the bottom of the tail to keep it clean on the journey.

The Journey

Some horses are better travellers than others, and it is obvious that those who find travelling uncomfortable will use a lot of energy during the journey. Although some horses never totally settle, many of the problems can be solved.

On Arrival at the Event

Always try to park on level ground. The horse will not enjoy standing on a slope all day, and the gas-powered fridge in your living compartment will not work properly – if you are lucky enough to have such luxuries! Leave enough room to tie up the horse at the side of the vehicle, and to lower a side ramp if necessary. In cold or wet weather, try to park so that wind, rain or snow does not blow directly at the horse and cause a draught.

In hot weather, try to find some shade where a through breeze can get to the horse. Lowering the ramp will also help to keep him cool. If the vehicle becomes very stuffy and hot, it may be better to unload the horse and to tie him to a loop of string attached to the ring of the headcollar (halter) or to a tie ring on the side of the vehicle. This is so that, if the horse pulls back violently, the string will break and prevent him from panicking. Never leave a

POINTS TO REMEMBER

- Always check that the horse has enough room within the partitions; he will need to find his balance by spreading his legs, and a restricted area may prevent him from doing this.
- A partition that is solid to the floor will prevent the horse from spreading his legs sufficiently, so ensure that the bottom third of the partition has thick rubber or plastic sheets which will allow the horse to move his legs.
- If the horse is travelling herringbone-style with other horses check that he can fit easily into the length of the partition, or he may have to travel with his neck bent in a most uncomfortable manner.
- Headboards ensure that the horse is not annoyed by his next-door neighbours, as long as each horse cannot get his head over or under the headboards.
- Make sure that travelling equipment is fitted securely. Bandages or rugs that slip will cause discomfort.
- If your lorry has a rug rack, secure the contents so that the horse below is not showered with bits of equipment falling down during the journey.
- A small haynet will help to keep the horse occupied and to take his mind off the journey.
- There should be a free flow of air through the vehicle, so that the horse stays at a comfortable temperature throughout the journey. Many vehicles are very poorly ventilated, causing the horse to sweat quite heavily. This is especially true when you are travelling with a full load, or if you become stuck in a traffic jam, as a stationary vehicle has a greatly reduced airflow compared with one that is moving. Trailers often have a good flow of air but can be a bit draughty, so make sure that your horse is warm enough.
- Bedding on the floor will help the horse to grip, and will encourage him to stale without his legs getting splashed. Any urine and moisture will be soaked up by the bedding, so the floor is less likely to become slippery. Skip the vehicle out each time the horse is taken off.

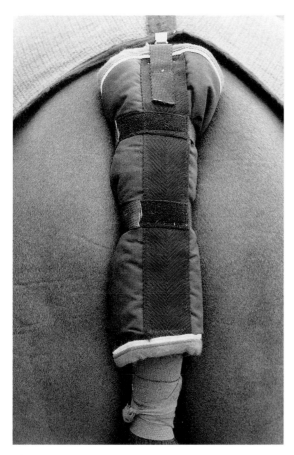

and warm him up. If the horse travelled with a haynet and you are going to compete in the next couple of hours, remove it. Lay out all your equipment so that you know exactly where everything is and can get at it easily. Good organization is particularly important if you are acting as your own groom and have no-one to help you. Having done all this, you are free to get your numbers and walk the course!

56 This tail guard is securely clipped to the rug to prevent it from slipping down (it could also be attached to the roller)

horse tied up like this unattended.

Offer the horse a drink if he has not had one in the last two hours, and check that he is a comfortable temperature by feeling his ears, shoulders and hindquarters, which should be warm and dry. A horse which has broken out into a cold sweat should be walked in hand to dry him off

SUMMARY

- Carry out a thorough safety check on your vehicle before setting out on a journey. Check the oil, water, tyre pressures, lights and indicators, and, if you are using a trailer, ensure that the hitch is in good order and that the safety chain is attached.
- A horse which is a nervous traveller may use a lot of energy during the journey. Make him as comfortable as possible by giving him adequate room to spread his legs for balance, and give him a small haynet to keep him occupied.
- In warm weather, ensure that there is a good airflow in the vehicle, particularly when several horses are travelling together.
- On arrival, park on level ground that is sheltered if the weather is bad, or shaded if it is hot. If the horse is unloaded and tied to the side of the vehicle, tie his rope to a loop of string so that, if he pulls back suddenly, the string will break.
- A horse which has been looked after and has travelled well will have preserved his energy and will be fresh and ready to compete.

7
WALKING THE COURSE

Depending on the nature of the competition, the severity of the course, your and your horse's experience and the time available, the course should be walked a minimum of one and a maximum of four times. At a hunter trial in the UK, where the course is normally fairly straightforward (in that there are few combinations to study, and most of the fences require only one jumping effort), one, or at the most, two walks will be sufficient. At a one-day event, where there are difficult combinations and technical fences to study, two walks are advisable so that you are familiar with every fence, approach and getaway.

At a three-day event, the course must be studied at least three times. On the first walk you will gain an idea of the fences; on the second walk you should study each fence and all its alternatives, including walking through the water where appropriate; and on the third walk you must check the line that you intend to ride at every fence, and also walk the alternative routes that you may have to take if things start to go wrong. (Refer to Chapter 5 for more detailed advice on choosing the best lines to take at individual fences.) Make a note of the layout of the start and finish areas, and where the scales are if you have to weigh out before your round and weigh in as soon as you finish.

The First Walk

At a hunter trial or one-day event

On the first walk, look at each fence individually and decide on the best place to jump it. Some fences will only have one option, so here, study the approach with regard to the terrain, the state of the going and any natural hazards which need to be taken into account, the siting of the fences and whether light, darkness or sunshine will have any influence on them.

When you come to the combinations, examine them from every angle before deciding on the line that is most suited to you and your horse. Having established this, walk back from the fence and make sure that you can pick up the line of approach at some distance from the fence. Remember that, when you are approaching on the horse, you will be going quite quickly, so you must prepare early enough for each fence (fig. 75). Think about the line of approach with regard to pace, speed and balance, and bear in mind the alterations you will need to make once you have landed over the previous fence. Make a note of the start and finish flags, and the amount of ground that will be available for pulling up when you have finished.

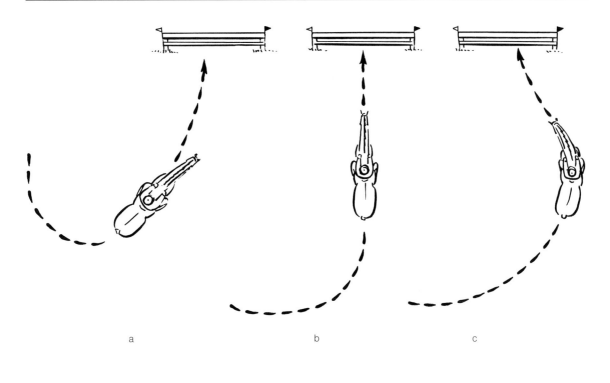

a   b   c

Fig. 75 The effects of correct and incorrect approaches to a fence after a turn
a If the horse turns in towards the fence too early, his inside shoulder will fall in, leaving him unbalanced
b If enough room is left for the turn to be made correctly, the horse's approach will be straight and balanced
c If the turn is made too late, the outside shoulder will fall out, causing loss of balance

If this is your only walk round the course, you will have to concentrate hard if you are to remember exactly where you are going. If you are able to walk the course again, all well and good. It often helps to familiarize yourself with everything if you can walk the course the day before the competition, so that you have more time to run through it in your mind. If you walk it just before you ride round, you have less time to tune your thoughts, although there is sometimes no alternative.

At a three-day event

The first walk round should give you the general idea and feel of:

- the severity of the fences and the alternatives
- the terrain, the state of the going and any natural hazards such as ditches or ridge and furrow
- the length of the course
- the siting of the fences, and whether the ground draws you towards or past each fence
- the influence that light, darkness and sunlight have on the fences
- the way in which the fences influence one another

Although you must take these points into consideration at this stage, you must try to look at the course from a 'first impressions' point of view. Studying it in more detail comes on the second walk round.

The Second Walk

At a hunter trial or one-day event

This is usually the last time you will see the course until you ride, although, if you have time, it is a good idea to watch riders negotiating some of the more complicated fences (unless of course you are first to go!). Walk the course on your own if possible, but if you do have company, make sure that you concentrate on the course and do not get distracted by conversation. You must be able to walk the proposed line that you will ride from start to finish, and, as you go, check that you are also clear on your line through the alternatives if this becomes necessary. Try to think of the 'feel' you will need when you are riding the course, so that you can plan ahead once you are riding it. Make certain of the start and finish flags, and of any compulsory turning flags on the course. Finally, go through the course fence by fence in your mind before you ride it.

At a three-day event

On the second walk, look at each fence in detail, at the different lines of approach, at every possible alternative way of jumping, and at the distances in the combinations. If possible, this walk should take place at the same time that you will be riding the course the following day, as this will give you an idea as to the influence that the light and sun will have on the fences.

From the start box, walk the most direct line to the first fence, bearing in mind that it should be jumped straight. The first two or three fences are usually straightforward, and designed to encourage the horse and rider to build up a good confident, balanced rhythm. If the terrain is difficult, you must be conscious from the start of how you are going to look after the horse's balance while maintaining enough energy for the jumping, as the ground may make it more difficult to find a good rhythm.

The first combination fence usually comes at about fence five. Walk every possible route, and bear in mind the consequences of crossing your tracks and the subsequent penalties you will incur. Check whether the fences are numbered individually, or whether the whole combination is one fence split into parts. This is important, as there are different rules on penalties depending on how the combination is numbered. Although you may be confident of finding a way through each combination that is suitable for you and your horse, remember that, on the day, those particular routes may not jump well, and another line or way through the fence may be more suitable **(fig. 76)**. Always bear in mind that a few time penalties are less expensive than twenty penalties for a run-out, refusal or crossed tracks, and much less expensive than sixty penalties for a fall. Continue to walk the most direct route between fences, and examine every combination that you come across in the same way.

The idea is to jump the single fences out of a balanced, rhythmic pace, so that the horse will be confident to tackle the more complex fences as he comes to them. When walking the course for second time, try to think of the influence that each fence will have on the next. If, for instance, there is a brush fence with a downhill approach and landing, and then, later, a coffin with a brush fence as the first element which also has a downhill approach and landing, the first brush fence should be jumped in balance and with confidence, so that, when you come to the coffin, the horse will be full of confidence even though he cannot see what is on the landing side.

The way in which you negotiate the first water fence will also influence the second. Wear wellington boots for the second walk

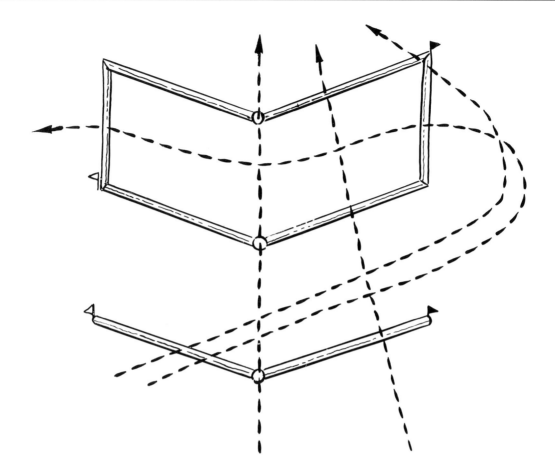

Fig. 76 It is vital to make a note of all the alternative routes at every combination when walking the course, in case your intended route cannot be taken for any reason

round, so that you can walk the line through the water fences. Do not just walk your intended line through the water, but also walk off the line, in case the water suddenly becomes deep or the bottom variable.

Towards the end of the course, be aware that the horse may be getting tired, making easier routes through fences advisable, but walk the more direct routes as well. Walk the last fence to the finish line and be sure to familiarize yourself with the pulling-up and weighing-in areas. There are also stopping points at various

intervals around the course, of which you must take note. If a red flag is waved at you near a stopping point, gallop past the stopping point and pull up without jumping another obstacle. When given the go-ahead from the official, re-establish the speed at which you were going prior to being stopped, re-pass the stopping point and continue on the course. The time during which you were stopped will be deducted from your total time taken on the course. If you ever fail to stop before jumping the next fence, you are likely to be eliminated and disciplined by the stewards.

It is a good idea to walk a three-day event course for the second time with someone who knows you and your horse, and whose advice you respect. They will often point out an aspect of a fence that you have failed to notice, and it is also helpful to be able to discuss ideas that you have for the fences.

The third walk at a three-day event

The third and probably final walk round the course should either be the evening before the cross-country or on the following morning, depending on which is the most suitable. If the weather has been bad overnight, it will be helpful to walk the course the following morning so that you can see how much the ground has altered. On this walk you must concentrate hard, so do not take somebody with you who will stop you from keeping your mind on the job that you have come to do. There is no point in spending months or years training for competitions only to blow your chances through not applying your whole mind.

From the moment you walk through the start, you must concentrate all your thoughts on the course, on how you are going to ride it and on what actions you will take if things do not go according to plan. You must walk from fence to fence on the line you are going to ride, and keep looking back to check that you are not walking a crooked line, especially when you walk the lines through the combinations. Try to walk the most direct line from fence to fence, remembering that you will be travelling at speed and so it must be a smooth line so that the horse can gallop within a rhythm. Cross-country courses

are often roped, so make sure that this has been done before your final walk, as there is nothing worse than planning a route to a fence only to find that the roping prohibits you from taking that line on the day.

The state of going can change enormously between your first and last walks, so make a mental note of how the ground will influence the horse's way of going and his jumping. If you have time on cross-country day, try to watch some of the more complex fences being jumped by the earlier competitors. If your chosen route through a combination is causing a lot of trouble, it will be as well to change to an easier, safer route. If it is not possible to watch yourself, ask a rider whose views you respect how the course rode for him or her. Try to find out how long it took to get to, for example, fences five and fifteen, and how long it took to get home from the penultimate fence. Be sure to ask someone who has jumped clear, not someone who has refused one or more times.

Riding across country is all about concentration, and having a well-worked plan as you go from fence to fence. You must also maintain a constant speed between fences, so that the horse covers the ground with an easy stride and uses up less energy. Bear in mind, however, that if you have to slow down to take a long alternative at a fence, it will take a little time to build up speed again, so think about this as you walk the course. At a three-day event, walk round as many times as possible but no more than once on the day, or you may expend valuable energy that you will need when you are riding.

SUMMARY

- A cross-country course should be walked a minimum of one and a maximum of four times, depending on the nature of the competition and the time available.
- Walk the course on your own if possible, so that you can concentrate fully and will not be distracted by conversation. However, on the second walk round a complex three-day-event course, where you will examine every fence in detail, it can be very helpful to be able to discuss your ideas with someone whose advice you respect.
- Try to walk the course at the same time as you will be competing on the following day, so that you can see the influence that the light and sun will have on the fences.
- Familiarize yourself with alternative routes at every combination, as well as the ones you intend to take, so that, if the horse feels nervous, you can take either one or two easier alternatives to restore his confidence. Remember that a few time penalties are better than a refusal or a fall.
- If you have walked the course the previous day but the weather has been bad overnight, it will be helpful to walk round again in the morning, so that you can see how much the ground has altered. Do not walk the course more than once on the day, as you will need to conserve your energy.
- On cross-country day, try to watch earlier competitors jumping some of the more complex fences. If a route through a fence is causing a lot of trouble, you will be wise to avoid it.

BEFORE, DURING AND AFTER THE CROSS COUNTRY

Getting ready

When you return to the horse, offer him another drink. If it is a very hot day, he could become dehydrated, and there is more good done than bad by offering him a couple of mouthfuls of water. You should have organized all your equipment on arrival at the competition, but fill your washing-down and drinking buckets with water if you have not already done so, and check that you know where everything is for your return with the horse once you have been round the course.

Allow plenty of time to get ready; if you start to run late you will become harassed and this will affect the horse. Those of you lucky enough to have a groom or helper should check that he or she knows what time the horse should be ready. If you get the horse ready before you change into your cross-country gear, put a rug on him so that he does not get cold. Never try to put studs in when the horse is in the lorry, as it is asking for trouble and some very nasty accidents have happened to people who have tried to do this. Even if it is pouring with rain, unload the horse, tie him up short enough to prevent him from eating grass, cover him with a waterproof rug and then put in the studs. The bridle can be put on after you have changed, but never tie him up by clipping the rope to the ring of his bit – always put the headcollar (halter) back on.

Warming up

You should allow half an hour for warming up the horse. Walk him for a few minutes, but if he will not settle, work him in a rising trot until he is quieter. It is better to work on a large circle if the horse is feeling fresh rather than riding at random around the warm-up area, or you will never gain his concentration. Have a canter on both reins in the large circle, but at this stage do not sit too heavily on his back or ask too much, as this preliminary warm-up is just to get the 'joi de vivre' out of his system. Walk him again, and then ask a little more by executing some transitions, on the circle initially and then on straight lines. Have another break, and then work at increasing and decreasing the length of the stride within the canter pace, which will help you to get the horse more engaged, active and attentive. It must be possible to alter the horse's stride length when riding cross country so that the horse can cope with the differing terrain and distances between the jumps.

After this warm-up on the flat, the horse

needs to have a few practice jumps. If the fences that are available happen to be uninviting and not really suitable for your horse's level of training, it is better to forget about them and to use the first two or three fences on the course to get the horse going. If there is a choice of fences, however, start over a cross pole in trot, then build up to an upright from canter, an ascending spread and then a true parallel.

Once the horse is going confidently, jump an ascending spread from a slightly stronger pace so that you can get into your cross-country rhythm. Remember to make the horse take bigger, more powerful steps but without losing the rhythm or the balance so that he can come to the fence with an even stride and jump it without having to alter his way of going. Jump the true parallel in the same way, but, to make

the fence a little more inviting, use a ground line set out from the take-off side to help you to jump it more accurately.

Jump the practice fences a few times, and then have another break. Just before you go around the course, build up your canter again to cross-country speed, have a final jump and remember to check your girths before you start.

Riding the course

As soon as the starter has counted you down and you set off, you must try to establish your cross-country pace by building up the canter within the rhythm (fig. 77). Try to find this rhythm by the first fence, but if it takes two or three fences, do not worry – just stay in balance

Fig. 77 Try to establish a rhythmic canter as soon as you set off on the course by sitting quietly and keeping your weight off the horse's back

with the horse. Jump the straightforward fences as easily as possible, and keep the horse channelled between your legs and hands so that, when the more difficult fences come, he is already jumping with accuracy **(57)**. Always get on to the line for each fence as soon as possible, and never let your concentration waver.

When you come to the combinations, jump them as planned, but, if you feel that your horse is not very confident in his jumping, take some easier alternatives to try to regain some confidence. If you jump a long route which takes you all round the fences, try to establish a rhythm for the turns so that you do not haul the horse around but incorporate the turns smoothly. Keep an eye on the clock if you are at a three-day event, but, if the horse is going well within himself, do not think of pushing him faster, as this may knock him out of his rhythm and he will then make jumping mistakes.

If you feel that the horse is getting tired but he is still jumping well, nurse him between the fences by keeping yourself as still as possible and, at the same time, keeping him together with your legs and upper body. If he starts to jump in a very laborious way, you should pull up. There is always another day, and, if you do not stop, the horse may make a nasty mistake, by which time it will be too late. Although a lot of very hard work goes into training and preparing a horse for competitions you must accept that things sometimes do not go according to plan. On these days, it is best to go home and start again tomorrow.

For more detailed advice on jumping the individual fences, refer to Chapter 5.

57 If the horse is balanced from the start of the course, he will already be jumping well and accurately, ready for the more complex fences

After the cross country

Having crossed the finish line, slowly bring the horse back to a walk. You should always slow down gradually, in a straight line and keeping a contact. The horse will be muscularly tired, and if the muscles do not function properly they cannot support the tendons and ligaments, so be sure to support the horse and not let him drop on to his forehand before he is in walk.

Dismount and loosen the girths and noseband. Keep walking the horse until he stops blowing: his respiratory rate should be below forty breaths per minute within ten minutes of finishing. If the weather is very hot, you can help him to recover more quickly by sponging water over his head at the poll and between his hindlegs, and by offering him a couple of mouthfuls of water every few minutes. In cold weather, put a rug on to keep his back warm, walk him and offer him small drinks. He may appreciate having the chill taken off the water by adding a little hot water from a thermos. Keep walking him until the respiration rate has dropped to about twenty breaths per minute.

The horse can then be untacked completely and washed thoroughly, but quickly and efficiently. Avoid getting too much water across his loins, as this can cause the muscles to seize up, and check for cuts and scrapes as you go. Remove excess water with a sweat scraper and dry the lower legs, heels and ears with a towel. Rug him appropriately for the weather, bearing in mind that he will not be dry, so a cooler is best placed next to his back. Remove the studs, pick out his feet, take out his plaits if necessary and treat any minor injuries. He can now be walked for about twenty minutes until he is totally dry and relaxed. By this stage he will hopefully have drunk some water – up to a bucket is quite normal. Electrolytes can now be added to the water at the recom-mended rate, to help him to recover from the exertion and to prevent dehydration. Offer him some grass, interspersed with periods of walking. Before loading the horse back on to the lorry or trailer, groom him thoroughly (weather-permitting) to remove any traces of sweat or dirt, and apply cooling lotion or a poultice to his legs **(58)**. Bandage his legs with a good layer of padding underneath **(59)**. Put on dry rugs if the weather has been wet and cold, or a sweat rug and cotton sheet for hot weather. Never leave the rugs unse-cured around the horse's belly or at the front, as it is easy for them to end up around the front or hindlegs on the way home.

In very wet weather it is essential to try and make the horse comfortable as quickly as possible. After the cross country, only wash the muddy and sweaty areas, and walk the horse as before, but with a waterproof rug over the other rugs. Grooming will be impracticable, but try to wash and pick out his feet before loading.

The horse can be given a hay net after he has been washed and bandaged, and a small feed of 1 to 2 kg (2 to 4 lb) can be given ninety minutes after the horse has finished his round. He will have expended a lot of energy, so use feed stuff from his ration that is high in energy and is easily digestible. Some people prefer to add the electrolytes to the feed at this stage, rather than to the water. Make sure that the horse can eat his feed undisturbed, and remove any feed left for more than thirty minutes so that he is not soured. Keep offering water, and check that he is warm enough and does not break out into a cold sweat.

Back at home

On arrival at home, trot the horse up briefly so that you have an idea of any stiffness or problems. Remove the horse's rugs and let him stale and roll, then brush off any bedding and, as long as he is totally dry, put on his rugs. Leave the bandages on until the morning, as they are offering support to potentially tired legs and will help to control any swelling. Top up the water two or three times that night if necessary and give a final feed no less than four hours after the previous one. The following morning, trot the horse up and check again for any heat, pain or swelling.

59 Plastic sheeting is applied over the poultice, followed by a good layer of padding. A stable bandage should then be wrapped over the top. Leaving the bandages on overnight will support the legs and help to control any swelling

58 A poultice or cooling lotion is applied to reduce any swelling or inflammation and to soothe tired legs

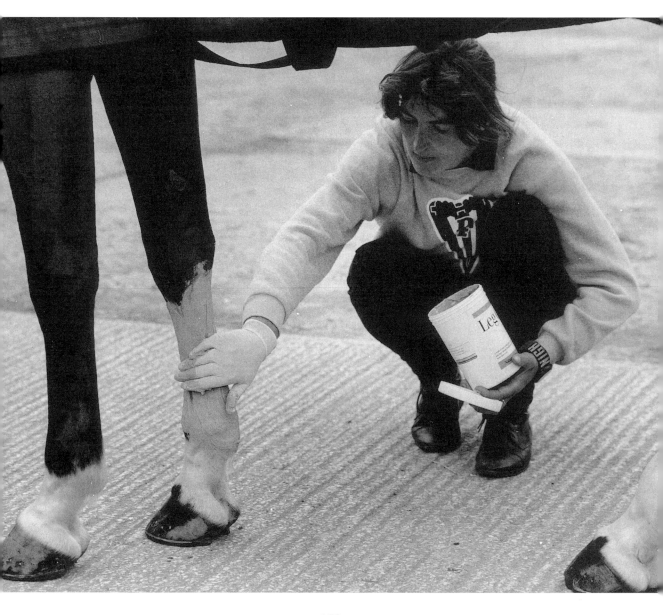

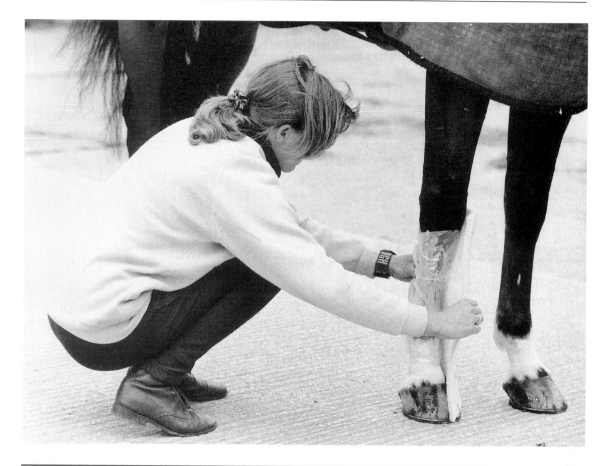

SUMMARY

- Never try to put in studs while the horse is in in the lorry or trailer, even if it is raining – this can be extremely dangerous.
- Allow plenty of time to get yourself and your horse ready. If you fall behind schedule and start to panic, your tension will transmit itself to the horse.
- Warm up the horse thoroughly before you begin by working him on a circle in walk, trot and then canter. Practise decreasing and increasing the length of stride, and jump a few straightforward practice fences to give him confidence.
- Try to establish your cross-country pace as soon as possible after starting the course by building up the canter within the rhythm. This will encourage the horse to jump the straightforward fences easily, so that he is already jumping accurately by the time you reach the complex fences.

- If the horse is going well, do not push him on faster unless you need to make up a lot of time, as this may knock him out of his rhythm.
- If the horse starts to jump very laboriously, pull up rather than risk a fall through tiredness.
- Make the horse as comfortable as possible after finishing your round. Walk him until he stops blowing, and in hot weather sponge his head and between his hindlegs to cool him down. Offer mouthfuls of water at regular intervals until he is completely cool and relaxed.
- Bandage the horse's legs for support and protection while travelling, and put on rugs if necessary to keep him warm. When you get home, trot him up briefly to check for any stiffness or other problems.

CONCLUSION

Always remember that you are one half of a partnership, and that, without your horse, you would not be able to ride across country. Always bear in mind the following 'do's' and 'don'ts'.

Do:

- look after your horse to the best of your ability and experience
- feed him in the best possible way with good-quality feedstuffs
- train and develop your horse to the best of your ability
- ride as well as you can
- make sure that your horse is sufficiently fit (this also applies to you!)
- introduce your horse to each cross-country problem in its simplest form
- have his teeth checked and rasped if necessary at least twice a year, or they may cause him discomfort
- plan a realistic fitness, development, training and competition programme, allowing plenty of time in case things don't go according to schedule
- build a firm foundation for both you and your horse
- swallow your pride and seek advice if you need it from a knowledgeable person. If you have help at regular intervals, many mistakes will be avoided, and prevention is always better than cure
- compete at a level well within your capabilities

Don't:

- treat your horse like a machine
- restrict his water EXCEPT after very strenuous exercise
- let his feet become overgrown and un-balanced, or allow the shoes to become very thin
- cause the horse stress if he is unwell (stress means taking the pulse rate over 100 beats per minute)
- over-exert him if he is unfit
- approach an unrealistic fence that you have no chance of jumping, as this will damage your and the horse's confidence
- approach a fence in a half-hearted fashion
- ask the horse to jump a combination that is beyond his level of training or where the distances are unfair
- frighten or confuse your horse by using obscure training methods that he may not understand
- overlook the importance of the road and basic fitness work

NEVER COMPETE if your horse:

- is not eating or drinking as normal
- has a change in temperature, pulse or respiration beyond his normal range
- has a dull coat or a glazed look
- has continuous discharge from his nose
- is coughing
- is shifting from leg to leg or from side to side when standing in the stable
- has any abnormal change in faeces consistency
- is fat and in soft condition
- has any heat, pain or swelling on any part of his body or legs

When dealing with horses, well-laid plans do not always turn out the way we hope they will. If things do go wrong – which they inevitably will – do not give up and take things personally, but seek good advice, find the cause of the problem and cure it. This often means going back to the basics, which is why it is so important to have a solid foundation from which to work at the start. When things go well, give yourself a pat on the back, but then start thinking about how to make them even better. If you think in this way, all your competition hopes and dreams may come true.

APPENDIX

CROSS-COUNTRY SCHOOLING VENUES IN BRITAIN AND THE USA

CROSS-COUNTRY COURSES AVAILABLE FOR HIRE

ENGLAND

County Durham

Ivesley Equestrian Centre
Waterhouses
Durham DH7 9HB

New Moors Training and Livery Centre
Evenwood Gate
Nr Bishop Auckland
Co. Durham DL14 9NN

Raygill Riding Centre
Raygill Farm
Lartington
Barnard Castle
Co. Durham

Derbyshire

Lea Hall
Lea Matlock
Derbyshire DE4 5GR

Snowdon Farm Riding School
Snowdon Lane
Troway
Marshlane
Derbyshire S31 9RT

Devon

Honeysuckle Farm Equestrian Centre
Haccombe With Combe
Newton Abbot
Devon TQ12 4SA

Westwood Farm
Crediton
Devon EX17 3PE

Dorset

Croft House School
Shillingstone
Blandford Forum
Dorset DT11 0QS

Leigh Equestrian Centre
Three Gates
Leigh
Nr Sherborne
Dorset DT9 6JQ

East Sussex

Crockstead Equestrian Centre
Crockstead Farm
Halland
Nr Lewes
East Sussex BN8 6PT

Essex

Carlton Equestrian Centre
Carlton Farm
Beehive Lane
Galleywood
Chelmsford
Essex CM2 8RJ

Sudbury Stables
Sudbury Road
Downham
Billericay
Essex

Wix Equestrian Centre
Wix
Nr Manningtree
Essex CO11

Gloucestershire

Summerhousee Equitation Centre
Hardwicke
Gloucester GL2 6RG

Hampshire

Decoy Pond Riding and Liveries
Beaulieu Road
Beaulieu
Brockenhurst
Hampshire SO4 7YQ

Rockbourne Ride
Tenatry Farm
Rockbourne
Fordingbridge
Hampshire SP6 3PB

Tweseldown Racecourse
Bourley Road
Church Crookham
Aldershot
Hampshire GU13 0ER

Herefordshire

Speedcote Equestrian Centre
Bartestree
Hereford HR1 4DE

Kent

Northdown Country Riding Club
Horton Kirby
Nr Dartford
Kent DA44 9BN

Lancashire

Osbaldeston Hall Farm Riding Centre
Osbaldeston
Blackburn
Lancashire BB2 7LZ

Leicestershire

Manton Lodge Stables
Oakham
Rutland
Leicestershire LE15 8SS

The Meadows Riding Centre
Kilby Road
Fleckney
Leicestershire

Mrs R. Purbrick
Chestnut Farm
Braunston
Oakham
Leicestershire

Lincolnshire

Grange de Lings
The Grange
Lincoln LN2 2NB

Hill House Riding School
Sand Lane
Osgodby
Market Rasen
Lincolnshire LN8 3TE

Norfolk

Mr R. Bothway
The Poplars
Wreningham
Norwich
Norfolk NR16 1AW

Northamptonshire

Moulton College
Moulton
Northampton NN3 1RR

Rushton Hall Farm
Rushton
Nr Kettering
Northamptonshire

North Humberside

Bishop Burton College of Agriculture
Bishop Burton
Beverley
North Humberside HU17 8QG

Northumberland

Mr and Mrs R. Charlton
Linnel Wood
Hexham
Northumberland NE46 1UB

Nottinghamshire

Newton House Farm
Newton
Bingham
Nottingham NG13 8HN

Wellow Park Stables
Rufford Lane
Wellow
Nr Newark
Nottingham NG22 0EQ

Oxfordshire

Achnaha Stables School
Rillington
Townsend Lane
Marsh Gibbon
Bicester
Oxon OX6 0EY

Mrs V. Haigh
Home Farm
Charlton
Wantage
Oxon OX12 7HE

Lyneham Heath Farm
Lyneham
Oxford OX 6QQ

Rycote Farms
Milton Common
Oxford OX9 2PE

UK Chasers
Otmoor Lane
Beckley
Oxford OX3 9TD

Shropshire

Tong Riding Centre
Church Farm
Tong
Shifnal
Salop
Shropshire TF11 8DW

Somerset

Stockland Lovell Manor
Coultings
Fiddington
Bridgwater
Somerset TA5 1JJ

Windmill Hill Equestrian Centre
Ashill
Nr Ilminster
Somerset TA19 9NT

Staffordshire

Offley Brook Stables
Heath House
Offley Brook
Eccleshall
Staffordshire ST21 6HA

Suffolk

Mrs Marilyn Chapman
Claredown Farm
Belchamp St Paul
Sudbury
Suffolk CO10 7DW

Uggleshall Manor Farm
Uggleshall
Beccles
Suffolk NR34 8BD

Surrey

Churchill Equine Care Centre
Grants Lane
Limpsfield
Surrey RH8 0RH

Dunsfold Ryse Stables
Dunsfold Ryse
Chiddingfold
Surrey GU8 4YA

South Eastern Toll Rides
Long Acres Farm
Newchapel Road
Lingfield
Surrey RH7 6LE

Warwickshire

Mr and Mrs H. Johnson
Red House Farm
Campion Hills
Leamington Spa
Warwickshire CV32 7UA

West Midlands

Kingswood Equestrian Club
Kingswood Lodge
Country Lane
Albrighton
Nr Wolverhampton
West Midlands WV7 3AH

Wiltshire

Mr N. Bush
Ebbdown Farm
North Wraxall
Chippenham
Wiltshire SN14 7AT

Pewsey Vale Riding Centre
Church Farm
Stanton St Bernard
Marlborough
Wiltshire SN8 4LJ

Savernake Forest Horse Trials Office
Savernake Forest
Marlborough
Wiltshire SN8 3HP

West Wiltshire Equestrian Centre
Melksham Road
Holt
Nr Trowbridge
Wiltshire BA14 6QT

Worcestershire

Hillocks Farm Equestrian Centre
Cleobury Mortimer
Nr Kidderminster
Worcestershire

Kyre Combined Training Centre
Lower Farm
Sutton
Tenbury Wells
Worcestershire WR15 8RL

Yorkshire

Aldfield Stables
Aldfield
Nr Rippon
North Yorkshire

Beaver Horse Shop
Windmill Farm
Beckwithshaw
Harrogate
North Yorkshire HG3 1QZ

Eddlethorpe Equestrian Services
(Malton) Ltd
Eddlethorpe Grange
Malton
North Yorkshire YO17 9QT

Factory Farm
Emley Moor
Huddersfield
West Yorkshire HD8 9TE

Hawksworth Equestrian Centre
Hillings Lane
Hawksworth
Nr Guiseley
Leeds
West Yorkshire LS20 8EP

Rillington Manor Riding School
Rillington
Malton
North Yorkshire YO17 8LL

SCOTLAND

Braeside of Lindores
Newburgh
Fife

Burgie Eventing Centre
Burgie House
Forres
Moray IV36 0QU

WALES

Severnvale Equestrian Centre
Pill House Farm
Tidenham
Chepstow
Gwent

Tarinth Equestrian Centre
Rhianfa
Llanllechid Road
Rachub
Bangor
Gwynedd LL57 4RH

Trewyscoed Riding Centre
Florest
Nr Abergavenny
Gwent NP7 7LW

USA

For details of cross-country schooling days, contact the USA Combined Training Association's area chairman for the appropriate area, as listed below.

Area 1

Ray Denis
8 Lake Avenue
Georgetown
MA 01833
(Tel: 508-352 2193)

Pam Hodsdon (Assistant Chairman)
92 Hayes Road
Madbury
NH 03820
(Tel: 603-742 5406)

Area 2

Richard H. Thompson
Sea Horse Farm
231 Spring Road
RD #2
Malvern
PA 19355
(Tel: 215-640 0699)

Area 3

Arrington J. Cox
516 Santee Avenue
Columbia
SC 29205
(Tel: 803-252 3008)

Area 4

Jean Rosenfield
11215 Grandview
Overland Park
KS 66210
(Tel: 913-451 2177)

Area 5

Col. Allen D. Smith
P.O. Box 83
Paige
TX 78659
(Tel: eve. 512-253 6280; day 409-880 8677)

Alison Ramos (Assistant Chairman)
Rt. 2, Box 28
Blue Ridge
Tx 75424
(Tel: 214-752-5407

Area 6

Chris Bearden
5900 Old School Rd.
Pleasanton
CA 94588
(Tel: 510 248 2301)

Area 7

Cindy Burge
Route 2, Box 123
Medical Lake
WA 99022
(Tel: eve. 509-244 5718; day 509-244 9415)

Michael Cooper (Assistant Chairman)
26102 S. E. 235th Street
Maple Valley
WA 98038-6747
(Tel: eve. 206-432 1979)

Area 8

Bernard D. Mullady
550 North State Street
Westerville
OH 43081
(Tel: eve. 614-890 2081; day 614-523 1956)

Elizebeth Chilcott (Assistant Chairman)
10240 Eureka Road
Edithboro
PA 16412
(Tel: 814.734 5009)

Area 9

Janet Goodrich-Spear (Co-Chairman)
12400 Arapahoe
Lafayette
CO 80026
(Tel: 303-666 7434)

Mary Ann Miller (Co-Chairman)
P.O. Box 1685
Ogden
UT 84402
(Tel: day 801-399 5871)

Area 10

John H. Caskey
Route 4, Box 753
Flagstaff
AZ 86001
(Tel: 602-774 8671)

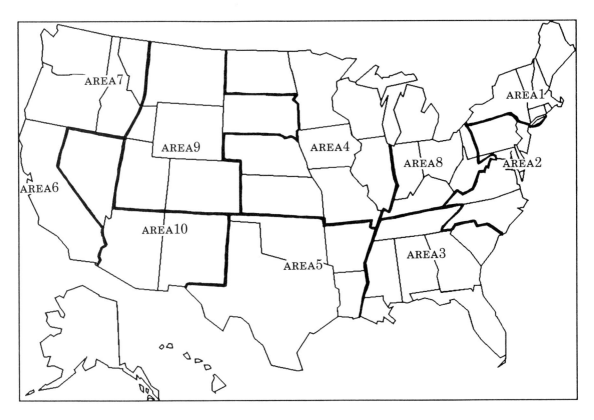

INDEX